THE LIFE
OF
GEORGE WASHINGTON

MARY L. WILLIAMSON
REVISED BY MICHAEL J. MCHUGH

Revised and edited by Michael J. McHugh
Layout and graphics by **imagineering studios, inc.**
Copyediting by Diane Olson

A publication of
Christian Liberty Press
502 West Euclid Avenue
Arlington Heights, IL 60004
www.christianlibertypress.com

ISBN 1-930367-91-0

Printed in The United States of America

PREFACE

More than two centuries have passed since the death of George Washington. Nevertheless, his accomplishments and godly character continue to shine with honor and dignity upon the pages of American history. Few men have done more to advance the cause of virtuous liberty than Washington. His legacy, therefore, is one that is worth studying and preserving so that each generation may know something of his honorable life.

George Washington lived during a period of great change and turmoil in North America. His great career began simply as a surveyor of lands for a wealthy landowner in the English colony known as Virginia. As a young man, he served in the English Army and fought bravely in the French and Indian War. After retiring to his estate at Mount Vernon, Washington served as a planter, a member of the Continental Congress, and also as a local magistrate. When the leaders of the English colonies determined to sever their political ties to the English crown, Washington took up the call to lead the colonial army in the War for American Independence. In the days after the fighting ceased, George Washington continued to serve his country during the formation of the U.S. Constitution and as the first President of the newly formed Union of States.

Regardless of the season or challenge, Washington never failed to live up to the call of duty, honor, and patriotic service. If young Americans living in the twenty-first century commit themselves to the task of imitating Washington's unselfish devotion to duty, then they will be well prepared to exercise the responsibilities of a people who have been set free to serve Almighty God. May God be pleased to use this brief study of the life of George Washington to strengthen and encourage a whole new generation of young patriots.

Michael J. McHugh
Arlington Heights, Illinois
2004

CONTENTS

The Boy and Young Surveyor

George Washington was born in Westmoreland County, Virginia, on Feb. 22, 1732. George was baptized in the orthodox Episcopalian manner less than two months later. The Washington family in Virginia came from England and their heritage may be traced back to the century following the conquest of England by William of Normandy, A.D. 1066.

The feudal name of the family, De Wessyngton, is found many times in the chronicles of England. In the lapse of time, the name simply became Washington; and in 1546 we find a certain Lawrence Washington living at Sulgrove Manor, Northampton. He was a man of property and distinction, being Lord Mayor of Northampton. The family continued to reside at Sulgrove Manor until 1606, when Lawrence Washington, the grandson of the Lord Mayor, removed to the village of Little Brington, where his home and tomb may yet be found. This place, which is sometimes called the "Cradle of the Washingtons," is only two hours' journey by rail from London.

In the mid 1600s, England was just ending a long and bloody civil war to overthrow the tyrannical Stuarts from their throne. The general who led the revolt to establish a more free and just England was Oliver Cromwell. This leader became Lord Protector in England from 1653–1658. The Washington family, like many wealthy upper-class English households, were royalists and, therefore, loyal to the Stuarts. While Cromwell was at the head of the government, the two sons of the Rev. Lawrence Washington, John and Lawrence, decided to come to Virginia. They arrived in 1657 and bought lands in Westmoreland County, between the Potomac and Rappahannock rivers—the region called the "Northern Neck." John, whom we afterwards find as Colonel Washington, leading the Virginia troops against the Indians, became a noted planter, a magistrate, and a member of the House of Burgesses. Augustine, his grandson, was the father of our hero, George Washington.

Augustine Washington is described as a tall man of noble bearing, with a fair complexion and fine gray eyes. He was a worthy man and commanded the respect of his neighbors. He married Jane Butler and settled down as a planter in Westmoreland County. In 1728, his wife died, leaving him four children, of whom only two lived to manhood. Two years later, he married Mary Ball, the beautiful belle of the Northern Neck of Virginia.

The young bride had passed her life quietly at Epping Forest, her father's country seat, where she had been carefully trained in all the domestic duties of her day. Though she had little book learning, she must have possessed a commanding character, as we are told that her sons, though "proper, tall fellows," were known to sit as "mute as mice" in her presence.

For several years after his second marriage, Augustine Washington resided in the old homestead on Bridges Creek, where George, the eldest child by his second marriage, was born. A few years later, the homestead was burned, and he moved to an estate in Stafford County, opposite Fredericksburg. Here he died in April 1743.

Besides her stepsons, the young widow was left with five children of her own—George, Elizabeth, Samuel, John, and Charles. To these children she devoted her life, being entrusted with the care of all their property until they should each come of age. A charming picture has been given us of Mary Washington with her children gathered round her, reading to them from her favorite volume, Sir Matthew Hale's *Contemplations, Moral and Divine*. This book, bearing her name written with her own hand, may still be seen at Mount Vernon.

Augustine Washington's large possessions were divided by will among his children; the home and the estate on the Rappahannock (Mount Vernon) was to become the property of George when he should reach the age of twenty-one.

During his father's lifetime, George went to a school directed by an old man named Hobby, who doubtless taught him to read, write, and work with numbers. When he was about eight years old, his half-brother Lawrence, who had been sent to England to complete his education, returned home an accomplished young gentleman. A remarkable affection now sprang up between Lawrence and his little brother, which lasted as long as the former lived and which had great influence upon the life of George.

Lawrence Washington must have inherited some of the military spirit of his ancestors, for we find him, when twenty-two years of age, raising a company and joining a military expedition to the West Indies, commanded by Admiral Vernon, for the purpose of punishing the Spaniards for interfering with British commerce. Thus it came about that George received his first lessons in military affairs. He saw the preparations made for the expedition and afterward heard of the war through his brother.

Fighting mimic battles was at that time one of the favorite amusements of the pupils of the old-field school where young George attended. George entered into this sport with much pleasure. He was commander of one army, while a schoolmate named William Bustle led the opposing forces, and it is said that George was always victorious.

After his father's death, George was sent to school to a Mr. Williams at Bridges Creek. Here he learned to draft all kinds of deeds, bonds, and mercantile papers, for his teacher believed in giving boys a practical education. His manuscript books, which are still to be seen at Mount Vernon, are models of neatness. This training was of great service to him later in life, as he was always able to draft legal documents with the skill of a lawyer. While still at school, he collected and transcribed fifty-four rules of etiquette which govern in good society. A few of the best rules of behavior compiled by young George were as follows:

#1–Every time you are in the company of others, you ought to show some sign of respect to those present.

#7–Stay away from people who constantly speak about other people behind their back. Do not get into the habit of prying into the private life of any person.

#9–If you visit someone who is sick, do not try to play the physician unless you have training as a doctor. Always speak the truth plainly, using the Bible as your guide. A sick or lonely person should not be told a false report about their condition. False hope breeds misery.

#13–Do not start arguments at the dinner table. Good humor makes any meal a wonderful feast.

#15–Respect your elders at all times. Permit them the first chance to speak when in their company.

#28–If you care to develop a good name and reputation, be sure to choose companions that have godly character; for it is better to be alone than in bad company.

#33–Do not envy the blessings of others. God gives to all that honor Him more than they deserve.

At this period of his life, George grew up rapidly into a tall and fit youth, and by practicing himself in all kinds of athletic exercises became noted for his agility and strength. A place is still pointed out at Fredericksburg, where, when a boy, he threw a stone across the Rappahannock River. He was also a fine horseman. A story is told that when only ten years old, he mounted a beautiful but vicious colt, which belonged to his mother and which no one could ride. The colt reared and plunged and ran, but the young horseman kept his seat. At last the animal made a furious plunge, struck his head against a wall, and fell dead. His companions were all frightened. What would Mrs. Washington say to the killing of her fine colt? Going to the house, George said to his mother, "Your sorrel colt is dead, Mother; I killed him." Then he told his mother just how it had happened.

Mrs. Washington was very upset at the loss of her colt, but after a few moments she said, "I am very sorry to lose my colt, but I am very glad to have a son who is not afraid to speak the truth."

When our hero was fourteen years of age, arrangements were made by his brother Lawrence for him to enter the navy as a midshipman. His mother at first consented to let him go, but after his trunks had been packed and the time came to say good-by, she was so deeply distressed that he gave up the idea and returned to school.

For the next two years, he devoted himself chiefly to the study of mathematics. He made a special study of land surveying, which in those days was a very important profession. He learned the "highest processes of the art," and spared himself neither trouble nor fatigue to become proficient. He made surveys in the neighborhood and kept field books in which notes and plots were entered with great neatness. "Nothing," says the historian Irving, "was left half done, or done in a hurried or slovenly manner. The habit of mind thus cultivated continued throughout life; so that however complicated his tasks and overwhelming his cares, he found time to do everything and to do it well."

In 1747, George left school and went to live with his brother Lawrence at the family estate at Mount Vernon. The latter had married Anne, the daughter of Hon. William Fairfax, brother of Lord Fairfax, and had settled on his estate upon the banks of the Potomac River. This estate he called Mount Vernon in honor of his beloved admiral.

While living with his brother, George was constantly in the company of the most intelligent and refined people, and by this association the manners of the home-bred boy received the stately polish of those colonial times. As Lawrence Washington was a member of the House of Burgesses and also adjutant-general of the district, there were statesmen as well as soldiers visiting at Mount Vernon. Their conversation relating to government and military affairs must have made a deep impression upon the mind of the thoughtful and manly boy.

When Washington was about sixteen, he was hired by Lord Fairfax to survey his lands beyond the Blue Ridge. These

lands had been taken up by lawless settlers, or "squatters," and Lord Fairfax now desired to survey the vast region and bring the whole under his own control. Though Washington was only a youth, he possessed the necessary vigor, courage, and ability to perform the task, and very soon the teenager was ready to begin the difficult undertaking.

In March 1748, Washington set out on horseback accompanied by George William Fairfax, a nephew of Lord Fairfax. They entered the Valley of Virginia through Ashby's Gap, a pass through the Blue Ridge, which then formed the western boundary of Virginia settlements. Here they found a beautiful region extending from the Blue Ridge on the east to the North Mountain, a spur of the Alleghanies, on the west, and watered by the beautiful Shenandoah river, which means in the Indian tongue "Daughter of the Stars." In his diary Washington dwells with delight upon the magnificent forests and fertile lands of this region.

The travelers first stopped at a kind of lodge where the steward of Lord Fairfax lived, about twelve miles from the town of Winchester. From there they followed the course of the Shenandoah for many miles. Usually they would camp out in the open air, but sometimes they would be invited to share the scanty fare of the woodman's cabin.

When, at last, having turned northward, they reached the Potomac, they found it so swollen by heavy rains that it was not fordable. Procuring a canoe, they crossed over in it, swimming their horses. They then traveled in a pouring rain forty miles up the river to the home of a Colonel Cresap. Here Washington saw for the first time an Indian war dance. A party of warriors appeared at the settlement and were induced by Colonel Cresap to dance for the amusement of his guests. The horrid appearance of the wild warriors and their terrible yells and whoops made a deep impression upon Washington, as he tells us in his diary.

Several weeks were now spent by the young explorers in the mountains of Frederick County, surveying lands and marking off the boundaries of farms. The weather was stormy and

their trials were many. Once, the straw in which Washington
was sleeping caught fire and he was awakened just in time
to escape being burnt. Again, their tent blew down and they
were driven out into the pitiless rain. In a letter to one of his
friends, Washington, wrote: "I have not slept above three or
four nights in a bed, but after walking all day have lain down
before the fire upon a little straw or fodder or a bear skin,
whichever was to be had, with man, wife, and children, like
dogs and cats; and happy is he who gets the berth nearest
the fire."

On one occasion, Washington and his traveling companion nearly froze to death on their way back to Mount Vernon. They had built a raft and began floating down the river,
dodging chunks of ice that had already begun to form on
the surface. As the two approached a tiny island, their raft
broke up and they were forced to swim to the nearby shore
through the freezing cold water. They could not start a fire
and were only able to stay alive that night by climbing up
and down trees to keep their body temperature from growing
too cold.

About the middle of April, Washington was again at
Mount Vernon. For wages he had received each day a dou-
bloon (between $15 and $16). He had done his work so well
that Lord Fairfax secured for him the appointment as public surveyor. His surveys were now recorded in the county
offices, and some of the lines run by him remain unchanged
to this day.

The description of the land possessions given by the two
young men was so pleasing to Lord Fairfax that he moved
across the Blue Ridge and took up his residence at the lodge,
known afterwards as "Greenway Court." The fine manor
house which he planned was never built, however, but
the old stone house in which the steward had lived served
for the entertainment of his guests. Here Washington was
always welcome, and here too he indulged in hunting and
other sports of the forest. Lord Fairfax was a man of culture
and varied experience and it is probable that Washington

derived both pleasure and profit from the companionship of his lordship.

Washington followed the occupation of surveying for three years and found that it paid him well, for there were then few surveyors for the vast tracts of country then being thrown open to adventurous settlers. The virtues of diligence and zeal were planted into the heart of Washington at an early age by his mother and by godly companions. The Book of Proverbs, chapter ten, rang true in the life of young George. "He becometh poor that dealeth with a slack hand: but the hand of the diligent maketh rich."

Throughout the beautiful valley, there are still homes which were built during colonial times that claim to have sheltered Washington when yet a young surveyor.

CHAPTER TWO

The Ambassador

Meanwhile, some of the most enterprising men in Virginia had formed a plan to settle the vast region west of the Alleghanies. You remember that both the English and the French claimed the country from the Great Lakes to the Ohio River. The French claim was based upon the discovery of the Mississippi by Marquette and Joliet in 1673. According to an unwritten law of nations, France had a right to claim not only the lands bordering upon the Mississippi, but also those touched by its tributary streams.

To oppose this claim, the English decided to purchase this disputed territory from the Indians. In 1744, a treaty had been made at Lancaster, Pennsylvania, between commissioners from Pennsylvania, Maryland, Virginia, and the Six Iroquois Indian tribes. By this treaty, the Indians gave up—for the sum of four hundred pounds—all rights to the land west of the Alleghanies, which region, they said, had been conquered by their forefathers.

It is true that the treaty and purchase did take place, but it is just as certain that the Six Nations or tribes at that time possessed not a foot of land west of the Alleghanies.

The time had now come for this great region to be settled. Both France and England began to make known their shadowy claims to it, and each of these nations prepared to outmaneuver the other by taking possession of as much land as possible.

In 1749, to gain a foothold in that country and to obtain wealth by its trade, an association called the "Ohio Company," was chartered, and five hundred thousand acres of land west of the Alleghanies was granted to it by the king of England. Both Lawrence and Augustine Washington were members of the company, and upon the death of the president, Mr. Thomas Lee, Lawrence Washington took his place. The company now began to make preparations to send out settlers.

In the meantime, the French under Bienville had taken possession of the country. He gave presents to the Indians, and after warning them not to trade with the English, nailed great leaden plates to the trees and buried others in the ground on which were inscribed notices to the effect that the land belonged to the king of France.

News of these proceedings was brought to the members of the Ohio Company, but they continued their preparations. In the fall of 1749, they sent Christopher Gist, a hardy pioneer from the banks of the Yadkin, to explore their possessions and to find out something about the native tribes.

Accompanied by several woodsmen, Gist went northward until he reached Logstown, the home of Tanacharisson, the Half King. As he was absent on a hunt, Gist pushed on to Muskingan, where he was well received and where a council of the Indian Nations was held. He afterwards visited Indian tribes by the name of the Delawares, the Shawnees, and the Miamis, all of whom expressed their friendship for the English and promised to attend a meeting at Logstown the next spring to make a treaty with Virginia. Logstown was situated a little below the site of the present city of Pittsburg.

Upon hearing of the proposed meeting of the western tribes at Logstown, the governor of Canada sent another embassy to the Indians, but with no success. The Indian leaders not only refused to listen to the French, but rejected the offered belt of wampum, the sign of peace and friendship. The embassy then left, making threats against the English and all others who might venture to trade upon those lands. In spite of all these warnings, Gist, under the protection of the Virginia legislature, surveyed the lands south of the Ohio River that belonged to the Ohio Company.

The French now prepared for war to protect their claims to land in North America. The English colonies also began to make ready for the contest which they saw approaching. There was quite a stir in Virginia, for the territory in dispute was within her boundaries. The colony was divided into military districts, in each of which there was an adjutant general, with the rank of major, whose duty was to organize and equip the militia to fight.

Through the influence of Lawrence Washington, his brother George was appointed adjutant general of his district. The compass and surveyor's chain were now laid aside by George for the sword and horse. A veteran, Adjutant Muse, instructed the young officer in the art of war, while Jacob Van Braam, a fencing master, gave him lessons in the use of the sword.

LAWRENCE WASHINGTON

In the midst of this excitement, Lawrence Washington's health became so delicate that, by the advice of his physicians, he determined to pass a winter in the West Indies, taking George as a companion. They reached Barbados in the fall of 1751, and were charmed with the tropical fruits and balmly climate of the island. Here Washington for the first time visited a theatre, and here, too, he was taken down with smallpox. After an illness of three weeks, he was restored to good health. He then visited various sections of the island and enjoyed greatly the strange scenes of a tropical country.

Lawrence Washington's health did not improve as it had been hoped, so he determined to visit Bermuda in the spring. George returned to Virginia to escort his brother's wife to her husband at Bermuda. But before the plan could be carried out, his brother's condition had become worse and the invalid hastened home to die under his own roof. On July 26, 1752, at the age of thirty-four, this accomplished and noble-hearted gentleman passed away, beloved and lamented by all. His infant daughter was left heiress to his wealth, but in the event of her death and that of her mother, the property was bequeathed to his brother George.

While Washington had been lingering at the bedside of his brother, stirring events had taken place along the Ohio. The treaty had been made at Logstown with the Delawares, Shawnees, and Mingoes; and Gist had been instructed to build a fort on the east side of the Ohio, not far from where Pittsburg now stands. The Ohio Company had also established a trading post at Will's Creek (now Cumberland, Maryland.)

The French, however, refused to give up the territory, and by various means induced some of the tribes friendly to the English to join them. They had even advanced to Piqua, the great town of the Miamis, sacked the place and raised the French flag.

Hearing of these events, Governor Dinwiddie sent Captain Trent to warn the French not to trespass on British soil. Trent found affairs so threatening along the frontier that he became discouraged and returned home without having delivered his message.

As it was necessary to send another ambassador to the French, Governor Dinwiddie began to look about for a person better fitted for the task than the discouraged Captain Trent. George Washington was recommended as having the necessary courage and determination, and Governor Dinwiddie chose him at once for the mission. He was directed to go to Logstown and there interview the Half King and the rest of the sachems. He was to tell them his mission and ask for an escort to conduct him to the French commander. He was to deliver to the commander a letter written by Governor Dinwiddie and in the name of the king of England demand an answer. It was also his duty to gain all the information possible about the forts and forces of the French and also about the Indians.

Washington left Williamsburg on October 30, 1753. Going by the towns of Alexandria and Winchester, he pushed on to

Will's Creek, where he was met by Gist. He engaged the latter as guide and one John Davidson as interpreter. His old friend Van Braam and four frontiersmen also accompanied him. On November 15, the little party set out on their long and wearisome journey.

Winter had now set in with storms of rain and snow which rendered the trails almost impassable and the rivers past fording. After many hardships, they reached Logstown on November 24. The Half King was absent at his hunting lodge fifteen miles distant. Washington, however, sent out runners and invited the Half King and other chiefs to a meeting on the next day. The Half King came promptly and gave Washington much information about the French forts and troop movements.

The next morning, the chiefs came to the council where Washington made his first speech. He told them that their brother, the governor of Virginia, was sending a letter to the French commander and that he needed the services of some of their young men to guide his party and to guard them against the French Indians, who were on the warpath. He then gave the chiefs a string of wampum, the emblem of peace.

The Half King replied that they would help their brothers, the English, but that three days would be necessary to prepare for the journey. Washington protested at the delay, but soon found out that to hurry the departure would offend his strange allies. He, therefore, awaited their pleasure. After much discussion it was determined that, for fear of arousing the suspicions of the French, only the Half King and two others should go as guides.

So stormy was the weather that it was not until December 4 that they reached Venango, the first French post. There Washington was told that he must deliver the governor's letter to the officer at the next fort. A storm detained them at Venango for three days, during which time Washington gained much information about the French; and the Half

King and his brother sachems consumed more of the French liquor than was good for them.

On December 12, the party at last reached Fort Le Boeuf on French Creek, about fifteen miles south of Lake Erie. Washington immediately presented the letter of Governor Dinwiddie to the commander, Chevalier de St. Pierre. Two days later St. Pierre delivered his reply.

His mission having been accomplished, Washington now made ready to leave. The wily Frenchman, however, detained the party for another day, during which he did all that he could to win the Half King to the side of the French. It was a time of great anxiety to Washington, but at last he prevailed upon the Half King to start upon the return journey.

They had gone to the fort from Venango in canoes and now began their return in like manner. The creek was swollen and full of broken ice. Often the canoes were in danger of being dashed against the rocks, and again the travelers would have to leap into the icy water in order to draw them over shoals. At one place where the river was dammed by ice, they carried their canoes for a quarter of a mile across a neck of land. Finally, however, they reached Venango on December 22, and on Christmas Day set out for home.

The weather was bitterly cold and the earth was covered with a deep snow. The packhorses were weak from exposure and lack of food, and it was feared that they would soon die. Washington and his companions dismounted and gave up their saddle horses to assist in carrying the baggage. For three days they toiled on in this way, when Washington, impatient to complete his mission, decided to hasten in advance of the party by taking the nearest trail through the forests. Leaving Van Braam in charge of the party, he, with his pack upon his back and a rifle in his hand, stepped out into the wilderness accompanied only by Gist.

When night came on, they made a fire and rested for a few hours. Starting again long before day, they pushed forward until they reached a place called Murdering Town. Here they came upon a party of Indians and employed one of them to act as guide through the trackless forests which now lay before them.

After traveling some distance, they came about twilight to an opening in the forest. The Indian, who was ahead, turned suddenly and fired at them. Washington was startled, but, finding that neither he nor Gist was wounded, pursued the Indian and seized him as he was reloading his gun. Gist would have killed him on the spot, but Washington interfered and saved his life.

They took his loaded gun from him and made him march in front. Gist now concluded that it would be best to get rid of him; so Washington said to the Indian in a friendly way, "I suppose that you had lost your way and fired your gun merely as a signal. Now as you are near your home, you can go there for the night."

"Yes," said Gist, "as we are tired, we will remain here and follow your track in the morning. Here is some bread and you must have meat ready for us early tomorrow."

As soon as the guide had left them, they kindled a large fire and set their compass by the light of it. They then began their journey again. Fearing pursuit by the Indians, they traveled all night and the next day until nightfall, when they reached the Alleghany River.

After passing an anxious night, they arose in the morning to contrive some way to cross the river. At last, they determined to build a raft. Though they worked with all speed, they could not complete it before the sun had gone down. They launched it in the gathering darkness, and tried to push it across the river with poles. Before they were half way over, the raft was caught between cakes of ice, and in trying to get it loose, Washington was jerked into the water by the force of the current. Fortunately, he was able to grasp one of the logs and by his great strength to climb back upon the raft.

They were now unable to reach either shore. At length, they drifted near a small island on which they took refuge. Here they spent a most miserable night. The cold was so severe that Gist's hands and feet were frozen. When morning came, the river was so gorged with ice cakes that they easily made their way to the opposite shore.

Before night, they had reached the house of Frazier, an Indian trader on the Monongahela. They left these comfortable quarters on January 1, and arrived at the home of Gist on the next day.

Having bought a horse, Washington continued his way alone and reached Williamsburg on January 16. He lost no time in delivering to Governor Dinwiddie the letter of the French commander and in making a full report of his journey. The letter was evasive; it indicated, however, no intention of giving up the territory.

The report of Washington convinced all parties that the French would take possession of the Ohio Valley in the spring. It was published and sent throughout the colonies, and to the mother country in England, in order to arouse the people and make them take measures to resist the French.

It soon became clear that there would be war on the American frontier between the French and English soldiers and between various Indian tribes who sided with one of these two nations. Captain Trent was ordered to raise a company of one hundred men on the frontier, and then to march to the fork of the Ohio and complete the fort begun by the Ohio Company. Washington was sent to Alexandria to raise another company and to forward supplies to the British forces under Captain Trent.

The journey from Williamsburg to Fort Le Boeuf and back again was fully one thousand miles, across streams, through dense forests, and regions frequented by hostile Indians. The fidelity with which Washington executed his dangerous commission was the foundation of his future greatness and caused him to be regarded as the "rising hope of Virginia." George Washington's military career was now beginning to blossom.

CHAPTER THREE

The Lieutenant Colonel

Governor Dinwiddie now appealed to the governors of the other English colonies for help. He also convened the House of Burgesses and demanded a grant of money to equip troops and fortify the frontier against the French. The governors all sent excuses, but the House of Burgesses voted ten thousand pounds for defense of the disputed territory.

A regiment of six companies of volunteers was called out, and Washington was offered the command; but with his usual modesty he refused it, assigning as a reason that he was too young and inexperienced. Colonel Joshua Frye of North Carolina was then placed in command, and Washington was made second officer with the rank of lieutenant colonel.

With two of these companies, numbering in all about one hundred and fifty men, Washington at once set out for the new fort at the fork of the Ohio. While waiting at Will's Creek for baggage wagons, he learned that the French, after driving away the men sent to build and guard the fort, had strengthened it and renamed it Fort Du Quesne. Regardless of this bad news, Washington marched on, making a road for his baggage wagons and artillery as he advanced.

The Half King now sent two warriors to assure Washington that he was friendly to the English and to ask help against the French and their Indian allies. They were reported to be over a thousand strong. News was also received that another French force was moving up the Ohio River and that six hundred Chippewas and Ottawas were marching to join them.

One of the warriors was sent to Williamsburg to see Governor Dinwiddie, and the other was instructed to inform the Half King that Washington was on his way with a part of the army, and to invite the Indians to meet him as soon as possible. He also wrote to the governors of Pennsylvania and Maryland informing them of his perilous situation and asking aid. In a council of war, it was decided to march to the Ohio Company's storehouse at the mouth of Redstone Creek and fortify themselves. There they could watch the enemy and await reinforcements.

On May 23, this message came from the faithful Half King: "It is reported that the French army is coming to meet Major Washington. Be on your guard against them, my brethren, for they intend to strike the first English they see. They have been on the march two days. I know not their number. The Half King and the rest of the chiefs will be with you in five days to hold a council."

That evening, the French were reported only eighteen miles away from where Washington was situated. The youthful commander, therefore, halted in a place called the Great Meadows and threw up hasty fortifications.

Having been informed by the Half King that an advance guard of about fifty Frenchmen were lurking in the forest nearby, Washington immediately set out by night with a band of men led by Indian scouts to drive off or capture them. This was done with great promptness. Jumonville, the young French commander, was killed at the first of the attack. The balls fell thick around Washington, but he escaped unhurt. Only one of his men was killed and two were wounded. Ten of the French were killed and twenty-one captured. The prisoners were at once sent on to Governor Dinwiddie, at Winchester, and letters were forwarded to both Colonel Frye and the governors urging them to hurry to the front both men and supplies.

It was afterwards claimed by the French that Jumonville and his party had been sent forward by the commandant at Fort Du Quesne merely to meet Colonel Washington, to advise his return, and to assure him that the French government would not consent to the building of a fort upon territory belonging to France. If Jumonville had advanced on a mission of peace, it was very unfortunate that he did not approach Washington's camp under a flag of truce instead of lurking in the forest. The force was reported to Washington as the advance of the French army; and, as he had no reason to think otherwise, it became his duty to attack it. The affair created great excitement throughout America, France, and England; but under the circumstances, no blame could be attached to Washington.

But let us return to the camp at Great Meadows. Colonel Innes, who upon the death of Colonel Frye had succeeded to the command, had not yet arrived. The promised supplies were not forwarded; and to make matters worse, the Half King and forty or fifty warriors with their wives and children joined Washington. He completed the fort and called it Fort Necessity, from the hard times which had been experienced while building it. His little army in the meantime was reinforced by one hundred and fifty men, who had been under Colonel Frye, and by an independent company of one hundred men from South Carolina.

With these reinforcements, Washington continued his march to Redstone Creek. When about thirteen miles from Fort Necessity, the scouts reported that a large body of troops had been sent out from Fort Du Quesne to attack him. Coming to a halt, he held a council of war, in which it was thought best by all to retreat before such superior numbers. A rapid retreat now began. Washington and his officers gave up their horses to aid in transporting the baggage and ammunition.

When the little army reached Fort Necessity, the men were worn out by hunger and fatigue, and Washington was forced to halt, contrary to his intentions. He sent back to Will's Creek for reinforcements and supplies; but before they could arrive, the fort was surrounded on July 3 by five hundred French and one hundred Indians under Captain de Villiers, who was anxious to avenge the death of his brother-in-law, Jumonville.

Washington had exerted himself to the utmost to put the fort in a state of defense, felling trees and rolling logs for the barricade himself. When the French appeared, he drew up his little army outside of the fortifications to give battle, but the foe remained under cover of the forest, which was not more than sixty yards distant on one side of the fort.

Washington then retired into the trenches and a fierce fight was kept up until eight in the evening. "Scarcely since the days of Leonidas and his three hundred deathless Spartans," says the historian Trumbull, in his book entitled *Indian Wars*, "had the sun beheld its equal. With hideous whoops and yells the enemy came on like a host of tigers. The wood and rocks and tall tree tops—as the Indians climbed into them to pour down their bullets into the fort—were in one continued blaze and crash of firearms."

Nor were Washington and his brave Carolinians and Virginians idle. For a full nine hours they fought with so much spirit that their little fort seemed like a volcano, roaring and flashing forth sheets of death-bearing flame. At eight o'clock, de Villiers, discouraged by such resistance, sent a flag of truce offering to negotiate with Washington and his men on honorable terms.

The situation in the fort had become desperate. A pouring rain had set in rendering many muskets unfit for use and filling the trenches with water; besides, the ammunition was almost exhausted and the stock of food provisions low.

Knowing that further resistance was useless, Washington finally agreed to the terms proposed. His troops were to abandon the fort, but they were to be permitted to march away with all the honors of war, carrying with them their stores and baggage. He agreed also that the prisoners taken in the skirmish with Jumonville should be returned. Captain Van Braam and Captain Stabo were to remain with the French as hostages until the prisoners should be restored to their countrymen. De Villiers had promised that the Indians would not molest the retreating forces. That promise, however, was not kept, for some of the Indian warriors pursued them and harassed them severely.

When the regiment reached Williamsburg, a vote of thanks was given to Washington and his officers, and a valuable pistol was granted to each of the men who had undergone so many hardships. Though the expedition had failed, the bravery and good judgment of Washington were not questioned by his fellow countrymen. As Washington grew in his experience as a military leader, he gained valuable lessons in how to know when to risk the lives of men and when it was better to seek a peaceful solution to a crisis.

CHAPTER FOUR

The Aide-de-Camp

After a brief rest, Washington returned to active service with his regiment. Governor Dinwiddie directed him to recruit new soldiers so that his regiment would include three hundred men. While he was doing this, the governor received information that the French had become less watchful at Fort Du Quesne and that it could easily be captured by a band of resolute men. Accordingly, he decided to order a forced march across the mountains for the purpose of taking the fort at a single blow. He wrote Washington to set out at once for Will's Creek with such companies as were complete.

Washington fully realized the rashness of such an expedition with so small a force at that season of the year, and he did not hesitate to express his opinion to his friend William Fairfax, then a member of the House of Burgesses. The latter doubtless brought such influence to bear upon Governor Dinwiddie that the project was abandoned.

As the House of Burgesses had voted a grant of twenty thousand pounds for military purposes, the governor issued instructions that the army be increased to ten independent companies. Under this plan, no officer could rank higher than a captain. "This regulation," says Irving, "drove Washington out of the service, for he thought derogatory to his character to accept a lower commission than that under which his conduct had gained him a vote of thanks from the legislature."

Washington was also thoroughly upset with Governor Dinwiddie because he refused to give up the French prisoners in accordance with the agreement made at Fort Necessity. He had tried in vain to persuade the governor to return the captives. In protest to the governor's refusal, he resigned his commission and retired to private life.

His first care was to visit his mother and render her all the assistance due her from an eldest son. He then went to Mount Vernon, which upon the death of little Sarah, his brother's daughter, had become his property. Here he entered upon the duties and pleasures of a country gentleman with the same zest with which he had gone to war. But he was not permitted to remain long in seclusion on his beautiful estate.

The British government, at last aroused, determined to aid the colonies in resisting the advance of the French. Early in 1755, General Braddock and two regiments, each five hundred men strong with all the munitions of war, were sent to Virginia.

Four expeditions had been planned by the British. The most important of them was against the French in the Ohio Valley. It was to be commanded by General Braddock in person. Fort Du Quesne was first to be captured, after which he would proceed against Niagara and Frontenac.

Alexandria was chosen as the place where the troops should disembark and be joined by the colonial soldiers and their Indian allies. There the troops would encamp and rest while all the details for their march through the wilderness could be arranged.

From the heights of Mount Vernon, Washington looked down upon the ships-of-war bristling with guns, and the troop ships swarming with red-coated soldiers as they passed up the Potomac to the place of encampment. The fighting spirit of his forefathers again seized him, and he declared his desire to join the expedition. This desire was reported to General Braddock, who soon learned from Governor Dinwiddie and others that our hero, because of his character, his knowledge of the country, and his experience in frontier warfare, was the very man he needed to accompany him as an aide-de-camp in the coming war.

When an invitation to join the general's staff arrived at Mount Vernon, Washington did not hesitate to accept it. As volunteer aide he would receive no pay. In fact, the trip would be at great personal expense. On the other hand, his passion for military life could be gratified without loss of dignity; moreover, he longed for the opportunity of gaining military experience under the eye of so distinguished a commander as Braddock. He therefore went as soon as possible to Alexandria, where he was cordially received by Captain Orme and Captain Morris, the other aides of the general.

General Braddock was also most courteous. Washington soon found, however, that he was a stern military man, very proud, and one of the sort that could be taught nothing new. He had great contempt for the simple, poorly equipped American troops who looked so shabby next to the scarlet-coated English with their fine weapons and perfect drill. He would listen to no warnings about danger from Indian ambushes. "The savages may be feared by raw American militia," he said proudly, "but they are not formidable to the king's regulars."

After remaining at home for a few days to arrange his business, Washington hastened to Frederictown, where he found affairs in great confusion. The horses and wagons which had been promised had not arrived; neither was there a sufficient quantity of provisions for the men. In this dilemma, Benjamin Franklin, who had come to Frederictown to see General Braddock, undertook to furnish one hundred and fifty wagons, with four horses to each wagon, and fifteen hundred pack or saddle horses, all of which were to be delivered at Will's Creek by May 20. In the end, these wagons and horses were lost and Franklin was sued by the owners. But the government at last paid the debt, which amounted to about one hundred thousand dollars.

Having scoured the country around for provisions, Braddock set out for Will's Creek (Fort Cumberland) by way of Winchester. We are told that he traveled in great state in a chariot, and that when he reached Will's Creek, a salute of seventeen guns was fired in honor of his arrival. Says Irving, "By the 19th of May all of the troops had arrived at Fort Cumberland—the two royal regiments, increased to fourteen hundred by men chosen from the Maryland and Virginia levies, two companies of carpenters, or pioneers, a company of guides, the troop of Virginia light-horse, commanded by Captain Stewart, the thirty sailors detached to assist in dragging the cannon over the mountains, and the remnants of two companies from New York, one of which was commanded by Captain Horatio Gates."

A long halt was now made at Fort Cumberland until the roads could be opened and supplies collected. In the meantime, Washington was sent back to Williamsburg to collect four thousand pounds for the military chest.

Upon his return, he found General Braddock fretting because the horses and wagons had not arrived. Washington advised him to use, whenever possible, packhorses instead of wagons. But knowing as yet little about mountain roads, Braddock did not heed the advice.

Another cause of anxiety was the desertion of his Indian allies. They complained that they were slighted in not being consulted in regard to the war; and one by one they disappeared from camp, until at last only nine warriors were left.

At last, on June 10, the ill-fated expedition again began its onward march. The crossing of the mountains with the heavily ladened wagons was indeed a tremendous undertaking. When, on June 16, the army had reached Little Meadows, General Braddock had become so worn out and discouraged that he humbled himself sufficiently to ask the advice of Washington as to the best manner of proceeding. The latter, with great modesty, advised him to divide his forces, to leave one part as a rear guard with the baggage, and with the other to hasten forward in person to attack the fort. This plan was adopted. It was decided that twelve hundred men and ten field pieces should form the first division. The ammunition and baggage were to be carried on packhorses. Washington gave up his best horse for the public service and never had the animal returned to him.

While the army was encamped at Little Meadows, Captain Jack, a famous Indian fighter, with his band of rangers, made his appearance and offered the services of his men to General Braddock. The assistance of the scouts would have been invaluable to the general, but he replied with great haughtiness that he had experienced troops upon whom he could rely for all purposes. So Captain Jack and his rangers, highly indignant, shouldered their rifles and left the doomed commander to his fate.

Once more, on June 19, the first division of the army began its march. To Washington's disgust, however, it moved forward as slowly as before, taking four days to march twelve miles.

Just at this time, Washington was taken with a fever, and had to be left behind with a guard and Dr. Craik at the great crossings of the Youghiogeny River. But he was impatient to be at the front, and as soon as he was able, he set off in a covered wagon and arrived at Braddock's camp on July 8.

The army was now only seven miles from Fort Du Quesne, and arrangements were being made for the attack on the next day. Washington, who knew the nature of the country and the probability of an attack by Indians, begged that the Virginia rangers, being expert in Indian warfare, be placed in the advance. The request threw General Braddock into a great rage. He said that things had come to a strange pass when a young Virginian should presume to tell him, a British general, how to fight.

Leaving the general, Washington, who was still weak from his illness, mounted his horse and joined the other staff officers. He soon forgot his wounded feelings in the splendid sight before him. The army was marching in perfect order along the bank of the Monongahela. He said afterwards that he had never seen anything more imposing than the march of the army on that bright morning. All were dressed in full uniform with bayonets fixed, colors flying, and drums beating.

After crossing the river, the road led up a gradual ascent, and on each side was a deep ravine, concealed by trees and underbrush. In front was a working party supported by a detachment of three hundred and fifty men under Lieutenant Colonel Gage (afterwards general). They had just begun to ascend the hill, and Braddock was about to follow with the main army, when very quick and heavy firing was heard in front.

The two ravines before mentioned, after running parallel to the road for some distance converged until they met, and just at this point the French attacked the advance guard of the English. As soon as the attack began, the French and Indians extended their lines down the ravines and thus from the bushes and trees poured a murderous fire upon the English. The advance guard was driven back upon a regiment which had just come up. The terrible war whoop of the Indians was heard on right and left, and from the front, and the experienced troops of Great Britain saw their brave comrades fall on all sides by shots from an invisible foe.

Colonel Gage ordered his men to fix bayonets and form in line of battle. Then the order was given to charge and clear the ravines of the enemy, but not a man would obey. The whoops of the Indian warriors so terrified the soldiers that they shot wildly, killing some of their own men who were retreating from the front.

In the meantime, General Braddock ordered forward eight hundred men under Colonel Burton, leaving four hundred to guard the artillery and baggage. As the uproar continued, he himself rode forward and arrived just as Colonel Burton was forming his men to charge. Just then the troops in front fell back in great confusion upon Burton's command, which also gave way.

Braddock tried in vain to check the retreat; he ordered the officers to divide the troops into small bodies and to advance against the enemy. But neither entreaties nor commands could prevail upon the men to leave the main road.

The Virginia rangers alone broke ranks and fought the enemy in their own fashion. Washington begged Braddock to post the regulars behind trees; but to the last he persisted in forming them into platoons so that they were shot down by the lurking foe as fast as they went forward.

Throughout the deadly conflict, Washington displayed the greatest courage and presence of mind. The other aides had been wounded early in the action, and he alone was left to carry the orders of the general. Two horses were shot under him and four bullets passed through his coat. The Indians singled him out for death, but in vain. He rode on as if protected by an angel. Not long after this battle, an Indian warrior is reported to have said that Washington was not born to be killed by a bullet; for he had seventeen easy shots at him with his rifle during the fight and yet could not kill him.

At one time, Washington was sent to bring the artillery into action. The Indians had extended down the ravines, flanking even the reserves, and there too the greatest confusion prevailed. The gunners were stricken with fear and refused to serve the guns. A well-directed fire upon the ravines might have saved the day. Washington dismounted and wheeled and fired a brass fieldpiece with his own hands, but his example was of no avail.

In the meanwhile, Braddock remained in the center of the field trying to rally his men. Five horses were shot beneath him, but still he kept his ground, hoping to turn the tide of battle. At last a ball struck his arm and passed through his lung. As he was being placed in a cart by Captain Stewart, he faintly asked Washington, "What is to be done?"

"We must retreat," was the reply. "The regulars will not fight and the rangers are nearly all dead."

The order to retreat was now given, and the rout became general. Baggage, stores, and artillery were left behind. The flight continued after the Monongahela River had been crossed. About one hundred men halted near the ford of the river, where a hospital was established. Here Braddock was tenderly cared for with a handful of food and supplies.

Washington was soon sent in haste to Colonel Dunbar, forty miles distant, who commanded the rear division, with orders to hurry forward wagons and supplies for the wounded. The tidings of the defeat, however, had preceded him and all was in confusion. Colonel Dunbar retreated after having destroyed stores and artillery, worth not less than one hundred thousand pounds. Braddock died the fourth day after the battle, July 13, at the Great Meadow. Washington had returned from Dunbar's camp and was with him at the last. It is said that he expressed to Washington his regret at scorning his advice during the campaign, and left to him his favorite charger and his faithful servant, named Bishop.

He was buried before the break of day. Washington read the burial service. Some historians tell us that the grave was purposely located in the middle of the road and that the retreating wagons were ordered to pass over it, so as to conceal his resting place from the Indians. The spot is still pointed out by the residents of that locality.

In this battle the English had twenty-six officers killed and thirty-seven wounded, and over seven hundred privates killed and wounded. The French had only three officers and thirty privates killed, and as many wounded. The destruction of the grand army, from which so much had been expected, caused much excitement throughout America and Great Britain, and reproach is still heaped upon the memory of poor Braddock for his obstinacy and military conceit.

On July 17, 1755, Washington again reached Fort Cumberland, saddened by defeat and weakened by disease. After having been in service for two years, he found himself with very little money and poor health; yet the trying scenes through which he had passed proved to be a training-school to prepare him for greater deeds. He wrote a letter to his brother, John A. Washington, on July 18, 1755, following Braddock's defeat, in which he acknowledged the hand of God in preserving his life.

"As I have heard, since my arrival at this place [Fort Cumberland], a circumstantial account of my death and dying speech, I take this early opportunity of contradicting the first, and of assuring you, that I have not as yet composed the latter. But, by the all-powerful dispensations of Providence, I have been protected beyond all human probability or expectation; for I had four bullets through my coat, and two horses shot under me, yet escaped unhurt, although death was leveling my companions on every side of me!"

CHAPTER FIVE

Commander of the Virginia Troops

The frontier of Virginia was now laid open to invasion, and though Washington was still suffering from ill health and the depressing effects of defeat, his military labors were not at an end. As adjutant general of the northern district, it became his duty to put the frontier in a state of defense against the expected raids of the French and Indians. He immediately issued orders that the militia meet and drill, and that volunteer companies be formed.

The House of Burgesses met and, thoroughly alarmed, voted a grant of forty thousand pounds for defense. It also appointed George Washington commander-in-chief of all the Virginia forces and voted him three hundred pounds for his services.

As soon as his mother heard of his probable return to military life, she wrote begging him not to risk his life in another frontier war. He replied with great deference, but insisted that, if called by the voice of his country, it would be his duty to obey.

It seems strange that a man who had already twice suffered defeat should have been entrusted with the defense of the Commonwealth. "But," says a noted writer, "it remains an honorable testimony of Virginia intelligence that the sterling, enduring, but undazzling qualities of Washington were thus early appreciated, though only heralded by misfortune."

Washington was indeed the hero of his people, not because he had been victorious, but because he had known how to bear defeat. Having consulted Governor Dinwiddie, he hastened to Winchester, his headquarters. He then visited the frontier forts and took all possible measures of safety.

Now happened an incident which would have been ludicrous had it not been for the anxiety which it produced, and the evidence which it afforded of the state of panic prevailing along the frontier. Washington was on his way to Williamsburg, when he was overtaken by a messenger from Colonel Stephens, the commander at Fort Cumberland, bringing the news that a large body of Indians was advancing up the Shenandoah Valley, burning and killing as they went.

Washington returned in haste to Winchester, where he found the citizens in great distress and alarm. News had come that the Indians were only four miles distant. With about forty men, Washington rode forth and found to his great relief that the supposed enemy was only a few drunken troopers who had alarmed the people by yelling and firing off their pistols. The real party of Indian warriors, which had alarmed Colonel Stephens, had advanced but a short distance and then retreated across the Alleghany Mountains.

Washington now bent all his energies to the defense of the frontier and the drilling and discipline of both officers and men in the militia service. Many of the militia volunteers were rough and rowdy men that struggled with sinful habits, such as drunkenness and swearing, on a regular basis.

In the meantime, a dispute arose between Maryland and Virginia as to the possession of Fort Cumberland. It was agreed that Major General Shirley, who had succeeded Braddock in command of the king's forces, should determine the matter, and Washington was ordered to Boston to obtain his decision.

He set out for that place on horseback, accompanied by his aides, Captain George Mercer, of Virginia, and Captain Stewart, of the Virginia light-horse. These officers traveled in great style on fine horses and attended by their servants. Washington's commanding person, splendid horsemanship, and widespread reputation made him the lion of the party.

Arriving at Boston, he explained his mission to General Shirley, who decided that Fort Cumberland belonged to the king; and that, as Washington was a field officer, he outranked the Maryland captain, who claimed the command of the fort. So Fort Cumberland was again placed under the command of Washington.

As he passed through New York City, he met at the house of a friend Miss Mary Philipse, a lovely woman, whose fortune was said to equal her beauty. It is certain that she gained Washington's admiration, and by some it is claimed that he offered her his hand in marriage and was refused. It is more probable, however, that he was called away by military duties before his courtship had progressed far enough to warrant a proposal. Be that as it may, it is recorded in the chronicles of the times that Captain Morris, his former fellow aide to Braddock, eventually married this good woman.

Although for about two years the French and the English colonies had been at war, it was not until May 1756 that war was openly declared by Great Britain against France. The conflict in America, known in history as the French and Indian War, now burst forth with renewed violence. In this sketch only those movements in which our hero took part will be mentioned.

The year 1756 was one of great trouble and trial for Washington. As laws relating to the militia service were not strict, the commander-in-chief had much trouble in raising troops to garrison the forts and to drive off the enemy. He was also greatly concerned about the obstinacy of Governor Dinwiddie, who insisted upon keeping a garrison at Fort Cumberland. According to Washington's opinion, that fort, being in Maryland, was too far removed from the track of the Indians to protect Virginia. He succeeded, however, in building a strong fort at Winchester, which was called Fort Loudoun.

In an effort to raise both the moral and spiritual atmosphere of the Virginia militia troops that were stationed at Fort Loudoun, Colonel George Washington issued the following order on September 18, 1756: "The men on parade tomorrow morning at beating the long roll, with their arms and ammunition clean and in good order, are to be marched by the Sergeants of the respective companies to the Fort, there to remain until prayers are over." It is plain that the danger of an Indian surprise attack was a factor, as the men were sent to prayers under arms; also it is plain that Washington took it for granted that the officers would display some interest in spiritual things and was annoyed that they did not, for the next Saturday came a more pointed order: "The men are to parade at beating the long roll tomorrow morning at 10 o'clock; and to march as usual to the Fort to attend Divine Service. The officers are to be present at calling the roll, and see that the men do appear in the most decent manner they can." Every Sunday thereafter, the men were marched to prayers and in the middle of November attendance at the Sunday service was made a standing order for the future.

In 1757, Washington attended a meeting in Philadelphia between Lord Loudoun, the British commander in chief, and the Southern governors. At this meeting, he set forth the defects in the militia laws of Virginia and submitted several plans which he wished adopted. Only one of his measures was carried—that of giving up Fort Cumberland to Maryland, and making Fort Loudoun at Winchester the center of military operations in Virginia.

The great plan of operations outlined at Philadelphia by Lord Loudoun, the details of which are told in general history, was an utter failure, for Montcalm, the French general, proved himself more than a match for his British opponents.

While these disastrous events were happening, Washington was defending 350 miles of the frontier with only 700 men. So great were the toils and anxieties of his situation that he was again seized by disease and was forced to retire for a time to Mount Vernon. In consequence of his ill health, he was even giving thought to resigning his commission. Just then, Governor Dinwiddie's term of office expired and he was succeeded by Mr. Francis Fauquier. Mr. Pitt, who was now made prime minister of England, adopted many measures satisfactory to Washington, and, as his health was improving, he resumed his command at Fort Loudoun early in April 1758.

To his great delight, the decision was made to try to capture Fort Du Quesne. He was ordered to march with two Virginia regiments, nineteen hundred strong, and join the expedition under General Forbes, who was collecting troops at Raystown, in Pennsylvania.

While assembling his forces at Winchester, he found them in need of both rifles and clothing. As letters to the authorities at Williamsburg were of no avail, he went there in person to obtain the necessary equipment.

While on the journey, he was invited to dine at the home of Mr. Chamberlayne, on the Pamunkey River. There he met a young and lovely widow, Mrs. Martha Custis, daughter of Mr. John Dandridge. Her husband, Mr. Custis, a man of great wealth, had died three years before, leaving her with two small children.

Washington seemed to be impressed by the charms and grace of the beautiful widow. According to orders, Bishop, his military servant, led the horses around to the door as soon as the noontide meal was over; but his master lingered at this place of beauty and hospitality. The horses pawed and champed their bits, impatient to be off, and Bishop wondered at the delay. At last the steeds were ordered back to the stable, and not until the next morning did Washington resume his journey to Williamsburg.

This time he was determined not to let a good and God-fearing women slip away from his life. His stay at Williamsburg was short, but before he returned to his command, he had wooed and won the fair widow. It was agreed that their marriage should take place the next winter. Saying farewell to his betrothed, he again set out for Winchester, where he arrived on July 2, 1758.

The war in the North had been favorable to the English, and the French had been compelled to weaken the garrison at Fort Du Quesne. So Washington was impatient to press on, feeling confident that the fort could now be taken. But it was not until September that he received marching orders from General Forbes, who had been detained at Philadelphia by illness.

When about fifty miles from Fort Du Quesne, General Forbes, contrary to the advice of Washington, sent a body of eight hundred picked troops under Major Grant to reconnoiter the country. This detachment was ambushed and routed with great slaughter. The Virginia regiment, which had been sent forward under Major Andrew Lewis, lost in the fight six officers and sixty-two privates.

Washington, after having been publicly complimented upon the bravery of his men, was now chosen to lead the attack and to throw out scouting parties to repel any Indian movements. Thus, slowly were the soldierly qualities of Colonel Washington recognized by a British general. All went well with the advance guard. When it was within one day's march of the fort, the French commander decided to remove his men at night into boats, set fire to the fort, and float down the Ohio.

The next day, the colonial and British troops marched up to the deserted fort, and Washington planted the flag of England upon the smouldering ruins. The power of the French in the Ohio Valley was now broken, and the Indian tribes of that region hastened to make treaties of peace with the English.

During Washington's absence upon the last campaign, he had been elected to the House of Burgesses by the voters of Frederick County. At the close of the year, he gave up his commission and retired from military life.

On January 6, 1759, his marriage with Mrs. Custis was celebrated with all the pomp of colonial style. The writers of the time failed to record the place where the marriage was performed. Though they gave minute descriptions of the costumes imported from London, of the bride and groom, of the bridal party, and of the coach and six horses, in which

GEORGE AND MARTHA WASHINGTON

the bride rode after the ceremony, with the groom following on his favorite charger, they failed to say whether the ceremony took place at church or at the bride's home, the historic white house on the Pamunkey River.

CHAPTER SIX

The Legislator and Planter

Soon after his marriage, Washington went to Williams-burg, and took his seat in the House of Burgesses. Mr. Robinson, the speaker, took occasion to thank him publicly for his distinguished services to his country. Rising to reply, Washington blushed, stammered, and was too much overcome to utter a word. "Sit down, Mr. Washington," said the speaker, "your modesty equals your valor, and that surpasses the power of any language I possess." So graceful an apology for his weakness could not help placing the youthful statesman at his ease.

Washington was now only twenty-seven years old. His figure was commanding and his face handsome. The life which he had led in the open air had given a ruddy hue to his cheeks and vigor to his movements, and thought and resolution were written upon his brow. Such was the man who now retired to the quiet of domestic life after a youth

MOUNT VERNON

devoted to promoting the safety and growth of his beloved Virginia.

Washington's life was still a busy one. Besides his own plantation at Mount Vernon, he had responsibility for the large estates of his wife and her two children. We are told by Irving that he rose early, often before daylight when the nights were long; then he would kindle his own fire and read or write until breakfast. After breakfast, he visited on horseback the various parts of the plantation where work was going on, often assisting with his own hands. He dined at two o'clock. He took tea, of which he was very fond, early in the evening and retired for the night about nine o'clock.

From a private wharf on the Potomac River, he shipped the produce of his plantation to various ports. Upon the river, he also kept a fine barge, which was rowed by six hardy men. The flour ground at his mill at Mount Vernon was famous in its day.

Washington was an active member of the Masonic order and belonged to the lodge at Alexandria. He was also vestryman of two churches, Fairfax and Truro, and was a devout Christian. Both he and Mrs. Washington regularly attended the Episcopal church. Although George Washington was a sincere Christian, he was not, nor did he pretend to be, a learned theologian. If Washington was more thoroughly trained in biblical doctrine, he undoubtedly would never have permitted himself to become a member of the Order of Masons, with its false teachings and worldview.

In spite of his many duties, Washington found time for recreation. He was fond of fishing, hunting, and riding. He was not averse to dancing, and he was particularly fond of theatrical exhibitions. The family would sometimes go to Williamsburg and enter upon the round of pleasures and hospitalities for which that famous city was noted. The beauty of Mount Vernon and the reputation of its owner brought many visitors to his home, where they were entertained with true Virginia hospitality. Mrs. Washington and her lady visitors rode in a chariot with four black horses in the lead, but Washington always appeared alone on horseback.

His entire time, however, was not given to his personal affairs, for as judge of the county court and member of the House of Burgesses, he was still actively employed in public life.

On behalf of a company of enterprising gentlemen, he undertook to explore the area known as the Dismal Swamp, with a view to draining it and rendering it fit for cultivation. This great marsh in the southeastern part of Virginia is about thirty miles long and ten miles wide. With his usual energy and boldness, he penetrated its dark and dismal recesses and found in the center of it the "Lake of the Dismal Swamp," a sheet of water six miles long and three miles broad. The following winter, the company for which he had made the explorations was chartered by the Virginia legislature as the Dismal Swamp Company. This company soon began improvements based upon his discoveries and suggestions.

In 1763, a treaty between France and England closed the bloody French and Indian War. Settlers again began to push out into the western wilds. Peace and prosperity now smiled upon the colonies, and it was hoped that savage warfare was at an end. The conspiracy of Pontiac, however, again deluged the frontier settlements with blood; and scarcely had the Indian uprising been quelled, when trouble arose with the mother country.

The recent war in America had cost Great Britain large sums of money, and the government now thought that the colonies should help to pay the heavy debt. Accordingly, in 1764, Mr. Grenville, who was then at the head of the gov-

STAMPS USED IN 1765

ernment, informed the American agents in London that he would introduce during the next session of Parliament a bill for taxing America—which tax was to begin with certain stamp duties.

This raised a howl of indignation throughout the colonies. Massachusetts, New York, and Virginia each sent addresses to the king and Parliament protesting against such treatment. In March 1765, however, the Stamp Act was passed. It required that all deeds, bonds, newspapers and business papers of every description be printed with a special stamp bought from an agent of the British government. It was also provided that any violation of this law should be tried without a jury by any royal court throughout the colonies.

Previous to the passage of the Stamp Act, the Navigation Laws (1660) had closed the ports of the colonies to foreign vessels and compelled them to trade only with England, utilizing English ships. The trade between the colonies was also subject to duties; and all manufactures that competed with those of England were either suppressed or made to pay heavy taxes. In 1760, an attempt had been made to collect duties on sugar, molasses, and rum imported into the colonies from the West Indies. To assist officers in collecting these duties, a kind of search warrant, called a "writ of assistance," had been authorized. With one of these in hand, any petty constable could enter any place, searching for and seizing goods which were suspected of being contraband.

The enforcement of these laws produced great excitement, particularly in New England where most of the importing was carried on. In 1761, James Otis, and two years later Samuel Adams, made powerful speeches showing that the American colonies should not be taxed unless they were allowed to send representatives to Parliament. Very soon, the principle of "No taxation without representation" was firmly established in the patriot cause.

In the meanwhile, vessels of the British navy hovered around the coast, and almost destroyed the trade with the West Indies by seizing a large number of merchantmen bearing cargoes of sugar and spirits.

All of these proceedings had been pronounced unjust and tyrannical, but the news of another method of taxation, the Stamp Act, was like a spark of fire in a magazine of powder. "The very night," says the historian Botta, "that the Stamp Act was passed, Doctor Franklin, who was then in London, wrote to Charles Thompson, afterward secretary of Congress, 'The sun of liberty is set; the Americans must light the lamps of industry and economy.' To which Mr. Thompson answered, 'Be assured we shall light torches of quite another sort!'"

The resistance to the Stamp Act began in Virginia, whose people at once declared it an outrage upon their rights. In the House of Burgesses, Patrick Henry introduced five resolutions which declared that the legislature of Virginia alone had power to tax its people; and in the discussion which followed made an eloquent speech for colonial rights, closing with these warning words: "Caesar had his Brutus, Charles I his Cromwell, and George the Third ..."

"Treason! treason!" shouted the chairman.

"May we profit by their examples," added Henry. "Sir, if this be treason, let us make the most of it." The resolutions were passed with some modifications.

Lieutenant Governor Fauquier, amazed at the boldness of the assembly, dissolved it, and the delegates returned to their homes; but the war cry of freedom had been sounded and soon it reechoed from Maine to Georgia.

Washington, from his seat in the assembly, had heard the speech of Henry and had returned home deeply interested in public affairs. From letters to friends in England and his agents there who attended to the selling of his tobacco and the shipping of goods in return, we see that he had fully determined to oppose all taxation. To be brief, the colonists now gave the British government to understand that they would never submit to pay the stamp duty unless compelled by force of arms; and on March 18, 1766, the act was repealed.

Various other acts of Parliament continued to give causes of complaint. Duties were imposed on tea, glass, pasteboard, lead, and tin. The Mutiny Act was also extended to America, and a clause was added requiring the provincial assemblies to provide the British troops with quarters and to furnish them with fire, beds, candles, and other necessaries. The assembly of New York refused to carry out this law, and its power was at once suspended by Parliament.

In 1769, George Mason, a friend of Washington, drafted the plan of an association, the members of which were to pledge themselves not to use any article upon which a tax was placed. This paper Washington promised to present to the House of Burgesses when it convened in May.

Lord Botetourt, who had recently come over from England, opened this session of the legislature with great pomp, riding from his palace to the capitol in a royal coach and making his speech as if he were a king. The members then passed resolutions denouncing the imposition of taxes and protesting against the trial of any person outside of his own colony.

Lord Botetourt was filled with wrath at the passage of these resolutions and the next day at high noon dissolved the House. But the members, filled with firm resolve, adjourned to a private house, elected Peyton Randolph chairman, and proceeded to business.

Washington now brought forward the draft of the pledge drawn up by George Mason. This was signed by all present and sent throughout the country. The signers pledged themselves neither to import nor use any goods taxed by Parliament. This pledge was rigorously kept by Washington, who directed his agents in London to send him nothing upon which a tax was levied.

Washington and other fine gentlemen put on homespun American clothes, and the ladies gave up their much loved tea drinking. His only sister Elizabeth, known as Betty, had married Colonel Fielding Lewis, of Fredericksburg, who was an ardent patriot. Colonel Lewis was such a violent partisan of liberty that he could not endure to have tea used by the ladies of his family, so he locked up all that he could lay hands on. Mrs. Betty, however, must have reserved some; for one day, becoming very, very thirsty, and forgetting her patriotism, she brought out her tea caddy and was enjoying a cup of tea with a lady friend when her husband appeared upon the scene. Mrs. Lewis used to be very fond of telling how quickly their innocent mirth was changed to mortification, and how they promised never again to break the pledge.

We are told by George Washington Parke Custis in his memoirs of Washington that Mrs. Lewis was a most majestic-looking woman, and so strikingly like her brother that it was a common amusement to throw a cape around her and to place a military hat on her head in order to intensify the likeness. Then she resembled her illustrious brother so much that battalions would have presented arms and senates risen to do homage to the chief.

In October 1770, Washington made another journey to the Ohio Valley. This time his mission was a peaceful one. He had been appointed one of the Virginia commissioners to settle the military debt of the colony, and in company with his friend, Dr. Craik, he crossed the mountains and transacted the business to the satisfaction of all concerned. In 1773, he again visited the Ohio region for the purpose of exploring a route for a road to connect the Potomac and Youghiogheny rivers.

Upon his return, he found his stepdaughter, Miss Custis, extremely ill. Her health, which had always been delicate, at last succumbed to the ravages of cancer and she expired on June 19, 1773.

This was a heavy blow to both Washington and his wife. All their hopes now centered in her son, John Parke Custis.

This young man, being also of frail constitution and having a large fortune in his own right, was allowed to follow his inclinations more than Washington, his guardian, thought proper. His mother, of course, indulged her only son, and when he announced his engagement to Miss Calvert, daughter of Benedict Calvert, she at once gave her consent. Washington, seeing that opposition was useless, also yielded, and the young people were married on Feb. 3, 1774—before the bridegroom had reached the age of twenty-one.

In the meanwhile, Governor Dunmore had succeeded Botetourt, and public affairs were going from bad to worse. The tax upon tea still remained and the people still refused to use it. In order to reduce the large amount of tea thus left stored up in its warehouses, the East India Company, being exempt from export duties, sent large shiploads of tea to various American ports to be sold at a low price, hoping thereby to induce the people to buy it. But the import tax was still upon the tea, and the people were angry at this attempt to seduce them to pay it.

At Boston, citizens disguised as Indians boarded the ships at night and threw the tea into the waters of the bay. At Wilmington, N.C., a vessel loaded with tea was boarded in the open day by a band of resolute patriots who threw the whole cargo into the sea. At Annapolis, Maryland, the ship, *Peggy Stewart*, was burned with her entire cargo of tea. It soon became clear that the people were determined to show Great Britain that they would not buy articles which were taxed.

The "Boston Tea Party," as it was called, so enraged the British government that a bill called the Boston Port Bill was at once passed by Parliament. This bill closed the port of that city to all commerce on June 1, 1774. Nor was this all. Another law altered the charter of the commonwealth and decreed that its governor, judges, and magistrates should be appointed by the king. Still another provided that any person indicted for a capital offense should be tried either in England or in some colony other than the one in which it was committed.

In Virginia, the House of Burgesses convened in May. The rich planters and the legislators had arrived with their families, and the town of Williamsburg was preparing for a ball in honor of Lady Dunmore, who had just arrived from England. Just at this time, a letter came announcing that the port of Boston would be closed on the first of June. This news came like a flash of lightning from a clear sky. Nothing else was the focus of discussion. The House entered a protest, and a resolution was adopted making the first of June a day of fasting and prayer to God Almighty.

The next morning, May 25, the House was dissolved by Lord Dunmore. The members dispersed only to meet again in Apollo Hall in old Raleigh tavern. There they passed even stronger resolutions against King George III and his Parliament. They also proposed that a general congress of all the colonies be held and that the delegates elected to the next

KING GEORGE III

House of Burgesses should meet in Williamsburg on the first of August to appoint deputies for this general congress, to be held in Philadelphia.

The ball in honor of Lady Dunmore came off as planned (May 27, 1774). The rebellious Burgesses bowed low before Lord Dunmore and his lady, and danced the stately minuet to the strains of dreamy music; but when the dance was over and the lights were out, they turned to weightier matters.

The first of June was observed throughout Virginia as a day of fasting and prayer to implore that "God would arrest the evils which threatened, and give them one heart and one mind firmly to oppose, by all just and proper means, every injury to American rights." Flags draped in crepe were hung at half-mast and funeral bells were tolled.

Washington states in his diary that he kept the fast and attended divine services. Being well-informed about military affairs, he must have been fully aware of the odds against the colonies. Less than three million people were preparing to oppose the most powerful nation of the world. They were without money and the munitions of war, and could rely only upon their own brave hearts and the help of God. But they had thrown down the gauntlet and were resolved not to endure taxation unless they were allowed to send representatives to Parliament. Washington, with many others, hoped that the misery produced in Great Britain by the refusal of the colonies to buy British goods would lead Parliament to a sense of justice before it was too late.

Events surrounding the movement for independence for the colonies unfolded in rapid succession. The proposed convention met at Williamsburg on August 1, 1774. It was composed of the best men of Virginia. In presenting the resolutions passed in his county of Fairfax, Washington made a truly patriotic speech. "I am ready," said he, "to raise one thousand men at my own expense and march to the relief of Boston."

The delegates appointed from Virginia to the general Congress were Peyton Randolph, Benjamin Harrison, Patrick Henry, Richard Bland, Richard Henry Lee, Edmund Pendleton, and George Washington.

On Monday, September 5, 1774, the first Continental Congress met at Philadelphia. "It is such an assembly," wrote John Adams, "as never before came together of a sudden in any part of the world." All of the colonies were represented except Georgia. The action of this Congress was calm and deliberate. Peyton Randolph was elected president and Charles Thompson, secretary.

One address was sent to the king, a second to the English people, and a third to the people of Canada. The colonists were not yet ready for independence, but they asked for a redress of grievances. They also resolved to hold no commercial trading with Great Britain until their concerns were properly addressed.

PATRICK HENRY

Patrick Henry, upon being asked whom he considered the greatest man in the Congress, said, "If you speak of eloquence, Mr. Rutledge, of South Carolina, is by far the greatest orator; but if you speak of solid information and sound judgment, Colonel Washington is by far the greatest man on that floor." This testimony from so great a man speaks volumes regarding Washington's character.

At the close of Congress, Washington lost no time in returning to Mount Vernon, for Mrs. Washington was alone and impatient at his continued absence.

Meanwhile, events moved rapidly in Massachusetts. A fleet and ten thousand soldiers had been sent from England to General Gage at Boston, with orders to put down the colonists by force. Boston Neck was seized by the British and the military stores at Cambridge and Charlestown were removed to Boston, and the legislature was ordered to disperse. Instead of obeying this order, however, the members voted to raise and equip an army of twelve thousand men, and also sent a protest to General Gage calling him to account for his actions.

The news of the state of affairs at Boston spread throughout the colonies, and, making common cause with that long-suffering town, they flew to arms. In Virginia, during the winter and spring of 1775, Washington was frequently called from home to review companies of volunteers and give them military advice.

In March 1775, he attended as a delegate from Fairfax the second Virginia convention, which was held in St. John's Church, Richmond. There Patrick Henry delivered the grandest of all his orations, ending with these words, "Give me liberty, or give me death!" He succeeded by his eloquence in carrying his resolutions that "steps should be taken for embodying, arming, and disciplining the militia." Washington sided with Patrick Henry and was one of a committee that drew up a plan for providing for the defense of the colony.

On April 18, a British force marched out of Boston to Concord to destroy or capture some arms and ammunition that belonged to the colony. Early the next morning, a company of armed colonists, known as "minutemen," met the British advance guard at Lexington. The British opened fire, and in a short time the colonists were dispersed with a loss of sixteen killed or wounded. The British marched on to Concord where they had a skirmish with another band of minutemen. After destroying five hundred pounds of bullets at Concord, they retreated, closely pursued to Boston. Men now armed themselves and flocked to that city. Within a few days, an army of

LINE OF THE MINUTE MEN
APRIL 19   1775
STAND YOUR GROUND
DONT FIRE UNLESS FIRED UPON
BUT IF THEY MEAN TO HAVE A WAR
LET IT BEGIN HERE
CAPTAIN PARKER

ten thousand patriotic soldiers had surrounded it and were threatening to cut off the British army from its provisions.

The news of the battle of Lexington was carried speedily throughout all the colonies, and the whole country was fired with the "passion of war." The news reached Virginia at a time when she was involved in trouble similar to that in Massachusetts. Lord Dunmore had seized all of the powder in the "Old Magazine" at Williamsburg, and removed it to the man-of-war *Magdalen*, lying in the James River. Patrick Henry advanced towards the capital at the head of a band of resolute men. Lord Dunmore was so afraid of these patriots that he paid three hundred and thirty pounds for the powder that he took. He and his family at last took refuge on board the man-of-war *Fowey* and never returned to Williamsburg.

Washington was preparing to attend the meeting of the second Congress at Philadelphia, when the tidings from Lexington reached him. Joining a rebellion against the mother country would be a great risk for a man of his wealth and influence, but he did not hesitate in his choice. He declared that he was a foe to all tyranny and that he was ready to die for the cause of liberty.

CHAPTER SEVEN

The Commander in Chief

On May 10, 1775, the second Continental Congress met at Philadelphia. As Peyton Randolph, the president, was obliged to return to Virginia as speaker of the Virginia assembly, John Hancock, of Massachusetts, was chosen to succeed him as its presiding officer.

JOHN HANCOCK

One of the first measures of this Congress was to send another petition to the king. The mother country

SAMUEL ADAMS

was still dear to the hearts of the colonists, and they yet hoped for concessions from the British government. But this hope was blasted when news came that reinforcements for the British had reached Boston and that, on June 12, General Gage had proclaimed martial law in Massachusetts, and offered pardon to all who would return to their allegiance, except John Hancock and Samuel Adams.

John Adams was now for "prompt and vigorous action." He headed the war party and, influenced by his eloquence, Congress began to prepare for the coming conflict. A federal union of the colonies was formed. In this union each colony had charge of its own affairs; but to Congress was given the

JOHN ADAMS

right of making peace or war, of regulating commerce, and of enacting laws for the common safety.

Just here, it is proper to note the weakness of the federation with which our nation began its existence. Under the agreement, Congress could collect neither revenues nor supplies necessary for carrying on war. These important functions were left to the individual colonies. Therefore, Congress and Washington, as we shall see, were constantly hindered and harassed by this fatal defect in the Articles of Confederation, which has often been called "no government at all."

Congress next voted to raise and equip an army of twenty thousand men and to issue notes to the value of three million dollars, bearing the inscription, "The United Colonies." The question of filling the important post of commander in chief was then taken up, and the eyes of all at once turned to Washington. Several delegates, however, thought that a New England man should be chosen. The army encamped around Boston was composed chiefly of men from that section of the country, and it seemed most fitting to select one of the distinguished men already in command. The matter was postponed until June 15, when John Adams rose and, in an eloquent speech, proposed that Congress appoint George Washington, of Virginia, commander in chief. The vote was then taken and he was unanimously elected.

When the result was announced, Washington arose and made a brief speech, closing with these words: "I beg it may be remembered by every gentleman in the room that I this day declare that I do not think myself equal to the command. As to pay, I beg leave to assure the Congress that as no pecuniary consideration could have tempted me to accept this arduous employment to the expense of my domestic ease and happiness, I do not wish to make any profit of it. I will keep an exact account of my expenses. Those, I doubt not, you will discharge, and that is all I desire."

A noted writer says of Washington: "He was now in the vigor of his days, forty-three years of age, stately in person, noble in his demeanor, calm and dignified in his deportment; as he sat on his horse with manly grace, his military presence delighted every eye, and wherever he went, the air rang with acclamations."

As it was necessary for the commander in chief to set out at once for the army around Boston, he could not return to Mount Vernon. This is a part of a letter which he wrote to Mrs. Washington just before starting on his journey: "I shall rely confidently upon that Providence which has heretofore preserved and been bountiful to me. I shall feel no pain from the toil or danger of the campaign. My unhappiness will flow from the uneasiness I know you will feel from being left alone. I, therefore, beg that you will summon your whole fortitude and pass your time as agreeably as possible. Nothing will give me so much sincere satisfaction as to hear this and to have it from your own pen."

Our curiosity as to Mrs. Washington's mind upon the subject is satisfied by the following extract from a letter to a friend: "Yes, I foresee consequences, dark days and darker nights. But my mind is made up; my heart is in the cause. George is right; he is always right."

While Congress had been adopting these measures of defense, stirring events had taken place in the North. The forts of Ticonderoga and Crown Point, which commanded communications with Canada, had been captured by Benedict Arnold and Ethan Allen, and vast military stores had fallen into the hands of the Americans. At Boston, the battle of Bunker Hill had been fought on June 17, 1775. Though this battle was a victory for the British, it had greatly encouraged the Americans. The result had proved that the colonial militia, armed with their own rifles

and fighting without discipline, were able to cope with the veteran troops of Great Britian; and from the blood of the slain patriots sprang a brighter hope of liberty. The news of this battle aroused great enthusiasm throughout the colonies. Everywhere the cry was repeated, "To arms! to arms!"

Washington set out from Philadelphia on horseback on June 21, 1775, accompanied by Major Generals Lee and Schuyler. They had gone scarcely twenty miles when they met a courier coming posthaste to inform Congress of the Battle of Bunker Hill. Washington listened with great interest to the report and inquired into all the particulars. When told that the Americans had not retreated until their ammunition was exhausted, he exclaimed, "The liberties of our country are safe!"

As Washington hurried onward, he was received with the greatest honor, and the most distinguished persons formed themselves into a bodyguard to escort him. The assemblies of both New York and Massachusetts went to meet him and to express their joy at his election. He answered with his usual modesty. From these speeches, it is plainly to be seen that Washington at that time did not aim at independence, but merely desired an honorable peace.

He arrived at Cambridge on July 2. As he entered the camp, the shouts of the soldiers and the booming of cannon informed the besieged British that some wonderful event had happened.

In the midst of these acclamations, Washington realized more than ever the greatness of his undertaking. He found the American army of fourteen thousand men "a multitude of people under very little discipline," scattered in rough encampments around the city for a distance of about twelve miles. The army was scantily provided with arms and equipment and its operations were greatly delayed by a lack of skillful engineers.

On the other hand, the British army, ten thousand strong, provided with all the munitions of war, was perfectly drilled and disciplined. It was also protected by powerful ships-of-war and fortifications constructed with the greatest skill.

Washington took formal command on July 3, 1775. His presence immediately infused great energy into the army. His engineering skill was brought into use, and new forts were thrown up and the lines so extended that it became impossible for the British to cut through them.

In the midst of these preparations, Washington found out that his ammunition was nearly exhausted. Couriers on swift horses were at once sent to various places begging immediate supplies of powder and lead. By God's grace, the British did not find out the state of affairs in the American camp and make an assault before supplies came. For nearly two weeks, Washington suffered the greatest anxiety. Supplies were finally forwarded from New Jersey and other places.

Washington now directed his attention to the expedition being sent into Canada by way of the Kennebec River. In the hope of persuading the people of that province to join the Americans in their struggle for liberty, Congress had formed a plan of sending a force to take Quebec. The main expedition under General Montgomery was to proceed by way of Lake Champlain; the other under General Benedict Arnold, by way of the Kennebec River.

Arnold's troops were detached by Washington from the army at Cambridge and consisted of ten companies of New England infantry and Daniel Morgan's mounted riflemen from the Valley of Virginia. It is not important to explain the details of this ill-fated expedition. Suffice it to say that, though well planned and boldly executed, it was in the end an utter failure.

After the departure of Arnold, attention was given to the enlistment of a new army. None of the soldiers in the American army were enlisted beyond Jan. 1, 1776, and, consequently, after that time they would be free to return to their homes. Congress therefore ordered that a new army be recruited and that as many men as- possible from the army in the field be persuaded to reenlist.

The siege of Boston continued during the winter with very little to enliven military life. Washington was almost

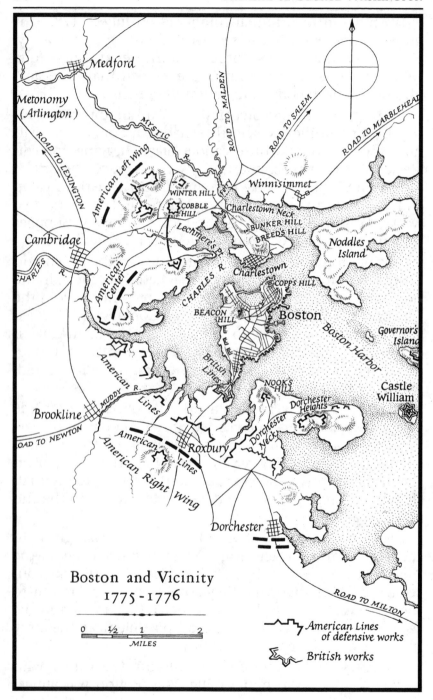

Boston and Vicinity
1775-1776

0   ½   1   2
MILES

American Lines of defensive works

British works

overwhelmed with anxious cares. The supply of powder was always short and the troops whose time of service had expired were leaving in great numbers. So few came to take their places that on Jan. 1, 1776, the army surrounding Boston did not exceed ten thousand men.

As Mount Vernon was thought an unsafe place for Mrs. Washington, the general wrote her to join him at Cambridge. She arrived in midwinter. We are told that she traveled in her horse-drawn coach, accompanied by her son, Mr. Custis. Her presence was quite a relief to Washington, for she presided at headquarters with dignity and grace, and attended to the social affairs of his military family.

As the spring advanced, it was resolved at a council of war held by Washington and his generals to seize Dorchester Heights and plant batteries in such a position as to command the city and thus drive the British from their fortifications. For two days, their attention was attracted by a constant fire from the American batteries. Then, on the night of March 4, a detachment of two thousand men with three hundred wagons was thrown forward and reached Dorchester Heights unperceived by the British.

The next morning, when General Howe, the new British commander, saw the forts on the Heights bristling with cannon, he exclaimed, "Those rebels have done more work in one night than my whole army would have done in a month!" Instantly, every gun which could be brought to bear upon the American fort commenced a fierce bombardment, and an assault was ordered. But a violent storm which arose beat such surges upon the shore that boats could not land that night. When the storm had passed, the Americans had rendered their fortress so strong that General Howe gave up all thoughts of an assault and found himself compelled to evacuate Boston.

After a parley, it was agreed that General Howe should retire from Boston unmolested, on condition that the city should not be injured by either plundering or the torch. On March 17, 1776, the whole British army went on board the fleet and sailed away; and on the 20th, Washington made his triumphal entry into the city.

The skill and patience displayed by Washington in the siege of Boston placed him at once in the highest rank of military commanders. The country was wild with joy at the expulsion of the British. Congress ordered a gold medal to be struck in honor of the event and also tendered Washington and the army a unanimous vote of thanks.

Expecting that New York would be the next point of attack, Washington began to concentrate his forces at that place. The patriot army now numbered about twenty-six thousand men, only half of whom were fit for service. The recruits were untrained, poorly equipped, and poorly supplied with provisions. Many of the patriot officers were untrained, and worse than all, disease was undermining the already thin ranks.

Major General Putnam was placed in immediate command of the army at New York. Under the direction of Washington, the work of fortifying the city and harbor was carried on with great zeal.

In the midst of these duties, Washington was summoned to Philadelphia to report to Congress as to the coming campaign. The king had paid no attention to the appeal of Congress; but in his speech to Parliament he accused the Americans of rebellion and declared that they had taken up arms to establish an independent empire. He also insisted that vigorous measures should be taken to subdue them.

An act was soon passed by Parliament prohibiting all trade with the colonies and authorizing the capture of American vessels and the imprisonment of their crews. Another act provided for the hiring of seventeen thousand German troops (Hessians), and the transportation of twenty-five thousand additional English soldiers to subdue the colonies.

These harsh measures convinced Congress that there was no hope of making an honorable peace and that it must prepare for a vigorous defense. Military stores were collected and powder was brought in from foreign countries. At Washington's request, Congress provided for a three-year enlistment

HESSIAN TROOPS

and offered a bounty of ten dollars to each recruit. A war office to take charge of military affairs was also established.

As soon as possible, Washington hurried back to New York to give his personal attention to the defenses and to the distribution of his scant forces. He was very anxious to prevent the British from getting possession of the Hudson River. To this end, he stationed General Schuyler and General Arnold at Fort Ticonderoga to watch events in the North and to collect a naval force on Lake George. He then directed his attention to the building of two forts above New York—on the Hudson River. They were called Fort Washington and Fort Lee.

Meanwhile, Congress at Philadelphia was discussing behind closed doors the question of independence. On June 7, 1776, Richard Henry Lee, of Virginia, moved that "these United Colonies are and of right ought to be free and independent States." On July 2, this resolution was passed, and on July 4, the "Declaration of Independence" was adopted by Congress.

INDEPENDENCE HALL

Everywhere the "Declaration" was received with joy; bells were rung, cannons fired, bonfires kindled, and processions formed. Though Washington foresaw the terrible conflict through which the Americans must pass, he hailed its passage with joy. He caused it to be read at the head of each brigade, and in his order of the day said:

> The time is now near at hand which must probably determine whether Americans are to be freemen or slaves; whether they are to have any property they can call their own; whether their houses and farms are to be pillaged and destroyed, and they consigned to a state of wretchedness, from which no human efforts will probably deliver them. The fate of unborn millions will now depend, under God, on the courage and conduct of this army. Our cruel and unrelenting enemy leaves us no choice but a brave resistance or the most abject submission. This is all that we can expect. We have, therefore, to resolve to conquer or

die. Our own country's honor calls upon us for a vigorous and manly exertion, and if we now shamefully fail, we shall become infamous to the whole world. Let us rely upon the goodness of the cause, and the aid of the Supreme Being, in whose hands victory is, to animate and encourage us to great and noble action, etc.

Great Britain was astounded by this stand for freedom. She had considered herself as bringing under control a lot of stingy and rebellious colonists whom she would punish severely for their obstinacy. Now, she found that a nation had sprung into existence—a nation willing to fight and die for its rights.

It is a curious fact that Congress should have taken this important step at a time when Great Britain was making a supreme effort to regain her dominion. Those grand men were building better than they knew. Looking back from the modern era, we see that they were laying the broad and deep foundations of a mighty republic that would someday become a beacon of hope and freedom to a dark world.

On July 9, 1776, General Washington issued the following order:

The honorable Continental Congress having been pleased to allow a chaplain to each regiment, with the pay of thirty-three dollars and one-third per month, the colonels or commanding officers of each regiment are directed to procure chaplains accordingly, persons with good characters and exemplary lives, and to see that all inferior officers and soldiers pay them a suitable respect. The blessing and protection of Heaven are at all times necessary, but especially so in times of public distress and danger. The General hopes and trusts, that every officer and man will endeavor so to live and act as becomes a Christian soldier, defending the dearest rights and liberties of his country.

The British now began to concentrate their forces near New York for the purpose of getting possession of that city and of the Hudson River, thereby dividing the northern colonies from the southern. Clinton and Cornwallis had arrived from the South and Admiral Lord Howe, the brother of General Howe, had come from England bringing strong reinforcements. General Howe now had an army of thirty-five thousand of the best troops in Europe.

GENERAL HOWE

Lord Howe had been instructed by his government to make peace with the Americans by pardoning all who would lay down their arms. The British refused to give to American officers their titles and treated them with the greatest scorn. Lord Howe sent a dispatch concerning the terms of peace to the American camp directed to "George Washington, Esquire." Washington refused to receive the letter which ignored his position as commander of the American armies. Howe then sent another communication addressed to "George Washington, etc., etc., etc."; saying that the "I and so forth" might mean any title at all. But Washington handed back the letter with the response that he would receive no communications which were not directed to him as commander in chief. We are told that Washington received the thanks of Congress and the nation for thus sustaining their dignity.

In the midst of the storm gathering around the patriot army at New York, good news came from Charleston, South Carolina. On June 28, the patriot army, under General Charles Lee, successfully repulsed the attack of a large British fleet on Fort Moultrie. Finding that no impression could be made by bombarding the palmetto walls of the fort, the fleet sailed to New York, having lost more than two hundred men.

Lord Howe now realized that there was no prospect of making peace with the Americans on the terms proposed by his government, and he at once began hostilities. Under his orders, General Sir Henry Clinton crossed over to Long Island with ten thousand men and forty cannon. The British landed without opposition and prepared to advance against the Americans.

The American army under General Putnam, nine thousand strong, had been stationed near Brooklyn to guard the heights which commanded the city of New York. The two armies were separated by a chain of hills covered with woods called the heights of Guan. Putnam expected to destroy the enemy upon these heights and stationed his troops accordingly.

To inspect the preparations that had been made to check the British, Washington crossed over to Brooklyn on August 26 and remained all day with General Putnam. In the evening, he returned to New York, for a night attack by the British warships was feared, and it was thought best that the commander in chief in person direct affairs near the city. It was a most anxious night for Washington. There were so many points that the enemy might attack, and so few men to defend them.

At break of day on August 27, the battle began. The attack of the British was gallantly repelled until the noise of battle was heard in the rear of the Americans. Sir Henry Clinton had found an unguarded road and by a rapid march had fallen upon their rear.

The patriots fought bravely and many of them escaped through the British lines, but many more were killed or taken prisoner. General Lord Stirling's division was in the greatest danger and suffered heavily. Some of his men escaped by casting themselves into the waters of the bay. These soldiers then swam across to Brooklyn. The three generals, Sullivan, Stirling, and Woodall, were taken prisoner, and about one thousand Americans were killed or missing. The British loss was slight. If General Clinton had followed up his victory and assaulted the works around Brooklyn, he would doubtless have captured the remainder of the American army.

From the thundering of the cannon and rattle of musketry about dawn, Washington knew that the battle had commenced. He hurried across the river and arrived in time to see the disaster, but was unable to prevent it. From a neighboring hill, he watched the retreat and dreadful slaughter of General Lord Stirling's command. Wringing his hands in agony at the sight, he cried, "Good God, what brave fellows must I have this day lost!" He could not even attempt their relief with men from the fort, for the garrison was already too small for its defense.

"Had he engaged all his forces in the action," says the historian Botta, "it is probable that the entire army would have been destroyed and America reduced to subjection." Great praise is therefore due to Washington for his prudence, which preserved both himself and his army for a happier future.

On the next morning, August 28, the British commenced firing at the fort, but did little damage. At midnight, a dense fog arose which hid the armies from each other during the next day. Seeing that he could not hold the position, Washington resolved to save the remnant of his little army by crossing the river that very night.

It was a perilous undertaking. Seven thousand men were to be withdrawn from the presence of a watchful foe "so near that every stroke of the spade and pickax from their trenches could be heard."

About midnight, the men began to embark. The boats moved noiselessly with muffled oars, and in six hours, aided by the darkness and fog, the whole army with its baggage and artillery had crossed in safety to New York. Washington remained at the ferry until the last man had embarked, though he had neither rested nor slept for two days and nights. This retreat is regarded as one of the most remarkable military maneuvers recorded in history, and reflects great credit upon the coolness and courage of the commander in chief. It must also be regarded as a heaven-born miracle, for if the Creator God had not intervened and sent a dense fog at precisely the right time, the colonial army would almost certainly have been destroyed.

At sunrise, General Howe discovered that the Americans had escaped, and great was his astonishment and chagrin. Long Island was now in full possession of the British, who were ready to attack New York.

Washington felt that with the means at hand he could not successfully oppose so powerful an enemy. He, therefore, removed all the sick and wounded to Orangetown in the Jerseys, and retreated with his stores and munitions of war to Harlem Heights, north of the city, establishing his headquarters at King's Bridge.

The condition and morale of the American army was now alarmingly poor. Until the defeat at Brooklyn they had flattered themselves that, because their cause was just, they would be protected by Providence. They had also persuaded themselves that personal bravery was better than discipline and had even sneered at Washington's endeavor to drill them according to European tactics. Now they had lost all confidence "in Heaven, in their commander, and in themselves."

Many deserted, while others did not reenlist when their time expired, and "those who remained were dejected and afraid of their own shadows." Indeed, a total collapse of the army was threatened. At this critical moment, Washington used all his powers of persuasion to revive the drooping spirits of his men. He wrote a stirring letter to Congress in which he begged that no more men be enlisted except for the duration of the war, adding that it would be impossible to gain independence with an ever-changing army. General Washington also sought to improve the quality of his military camps during this dark period by issuing the following order:

> That the troops may have an opportunity of attending public worship, as well as to take some rest after the great fatigue they have gone through, the General in future excuses them from fatigue duty on Sundays, except at shipyards, or on special occasions, until further orders. The General is sorry to be informed that the foolish and wicked practice of profane cursing and swearing, a vice heretofore little known in an American Army, is growing into fashion; he hopes the officers will by example as well as influence, endeavor to check it; and that both they and the men will reflect that we can have little hope of the blessing of Heaven on our arms if we insult it by

our impiety and folly; added to this, it is a vice so mean and low, without any temptation, that every man of sense and character detests and despises it.

To induce men to enlist, a bounty of twenty dollars was also offered by Congress and portions of unoccupied land were promised to the officers and soldiers. At present, however, Washington had only a few dispirited and ill-fed troops with whom to contend against a large and victorious English army. In this situation, he adopted the wise policy of harassing and retreating before his enemy without risking a general engagement. By this tactic, the Roman general, Fabius Maximus, had saved Rome when threatened by Hannibal almost two thousand years before. Washington has, therefore, been called by many students of history, the "American Fabius."

The British entered New York on September 15, and Washington withdrew to White Plains. Here the enemy attacked him late in October. The conflict lasted several hours without any decided advantage on either side. At night, the two armies lay within cannon shot of each other, the campfires lighting up the landscape with their lurid glare.

During this anxious night, Washington, expecting a bloody conflict on the morrow, removed his sick and wounded to a safer place. He also threw back the right wing of his army to stronger ground, doubling his entrenchments and throwing up works with usual skill. These redoubts were made partly of the stalks of Indian corn taken from a neighboring field and piled up with the earth clinging in masses to the roots. The next morning the Americans seemed so strongly entrenched that Howe deemed it prudent to wait for reinforcements.

On the next night, Washington made another move which greatly perplexed his watchful foe. Protected by the darkness and leaving a strong rearguard on the heights, he retired with his main army about five miles to the high and rocky hills around Northcastle. Here he again set to work to entrench himself, his chief weapons being at this time the "mattock and the spade."

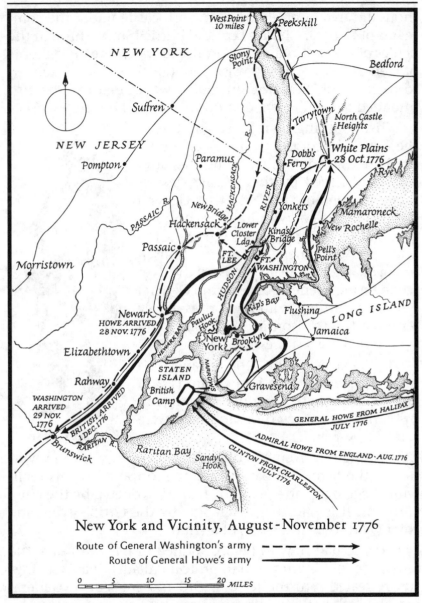

New York and Vicinity, August-November 1776

Route of General Washington's army – – – – →
Route of General Howe's army ⸺⸺⸺→

0   5   10   15   20 MILES

All was quiet for a few days, when during the night of November 4, a mysterious rumbling sound was heard, and when the dawn appeared, it was seen that the enemy was retiring towards New York. Washington now left seven thousand five hundred men at Northcastle under the command of General Charles Lee, and hurried south through the defiles of the mountains to Fort Lee to watch the movements of General Howe. There was no doubt that Howe intended to besiege Fort Washington, but it was feared that he also intended to send an expedition to capture Philadelphia.

When Washington reached Fort Lee on the right bank of the Hudson, just opposite Fort Washington, he found the latter closely observed by the enemy. He was much disappointed to find that General Greene, instead of withdrawing the garrison, had actually reinforced it with nearly one thousand men. Throwing himself into a boat, he had partly crossed the river when he met General Greene and General Putnam returning from the fortress. They reported the garrison in high spirits and sure of making a successful defense.

The next morning, the assault was made by the British in four columns, and after a fierce fight, Colonel Magaw and his garrison of three thousand men were forced to surrender.

GENERAL GREENE

Washington, from the opposite side of the Hudson, witnessed the fierce combat outside the fort and saw his men, while begging quarter, cut down and bayoneted by the cruel Hessians. It is said that, overcome by the terrible scene, he wept "with the tenderness of a child."

Fort Lee had now to be abandoned in haste. To save the remainder of his army and to protect Philadelphia, Washington retreated into the Jerseys. Orders were sent to General Lee at Northcastle to join him with his detachment, but he failed to obey.

Washington was followed leisurely by Cornwallis with all the "pomp and circumstance" of a victorious army. The American army was now reduced to three thousand men

without tents and clothing, and in the
midst of people hostile to the patriot
cause. Many of them had no shoes and
left blood-stained tracks on the frozen
ground. At last, they reached the Delaware River at Trenton, slowly pursued
by Cornwallis. By God's providence,
they were here favored by mercy from
Heaven. All the boats for several miles
along the river had been secured, and in
these the Americans crossed over.

LORD CORNWALLIS

Cornwallis came up soon after, and finding no boats on
the Jersey shore, he stationed detachments in Princeton,
New Brunswick, and Trenton. He expected before long to
cross upon the ice.

This was indeed the darkest hour of the patriot cause. The
army of Washington was too small to cope with the victorious force of the British, and the whole country was dispirited.
Congress adjourned in haste from Philadelphia to Baltimore,
for it was known that the British intended, as soon as the
Delaware was frozen over, to march on Philadelphia, capture
that city, disperse the little army of Washington, and restore
the authority of the king. But they had not counted upon
the wise measures of Congress nor the resolute resistance of
George Washington. He had no thought of yielding. About
this time, he wrote to General Mercer, "We must retire to
the mountains of West Augusta County in Virginia. Numbers will flee to us for safety. We will try a predatory war. If
overpowered, we must cross the Alleghanies."

Washington now sent General Mifflin and General Arm-
strong through Pennsylvania to arouse the people to fight in
the defense of their capital. He also ordered General Gates
to join him promptly with the best of the troops which he
commanded in Canada. This order General Gates obeyed at
once, reaching Washington's camp on December 20.

About this time, reports came to Washington that General Lee had been captured by the British. Though a fear-

less, dashing officer, Lee had become jealous of Washington, whom he maligned before Congress and before private persons of influence. It was thought by some that Lee himself had planned to be captured and that he afterward disclosed to General Howe the woeful condition of the Americans.

However that may be, General Sullivan now took command of Lee's division and hastened to join the army on the Delaware. Just before this, Washington had been reinforced by fifteen hundred militia from Philadelphia and five hundred Germans from Pennsylvania, so that he had now between five and six thousand men fit for duty.

He at once decided to attack some of the British forces, which were scattered along the Jersey side of the Delaware River. He was in New York, and Lord Cornwallis, believing the war to be over, was also there preparing to return to England. The river was now full of floating ice. In a few days, it would be frozen over and then the foe would cross over and march on Philadelphia. There were three regiments of Hessians at Trenton commanded by Colonel Rahl. Knowing that on Christmas night the Hessians would be drinking and celebrating, Washington determined to surprise them and if possible carry them off as prisoners.

The night selected for the attack was dark and stormy and it was with difficulty that the boats were driven through the drifting ice. Two divisions were unable to cross, but the third, under Washington and Sullivan, managed a landing nine miles above Trenton. Washington crossed over in one of the first boats and waited patiently on the icy bank until the artillery had been brought over.

It was nearly four o'clock in the morning before the troops began the march in a storm of sleet and rain. It was then impossible to reach Trenton before daylight, but it was equally impossible to return. So the little band of about two thousand pressed on and burst into the town from two directions just as the Hessians were beginning to stir in their quarters.

Washington commanded one division and Sullivan the other. The advance guard was led by a gallant young officer,

William A. Washington, assisted by Lieutenant James Monroe, who in later years was President of the United States.

Aroused by the approach of the Americans, the Hessians sprang into the streets and attempted to form in line. The American cannon began to roar and muskets to flash, sending deadly volleys into their ranks. Colonel Rahl was mortally wounded at the first onset. Having lost their commander, over one thousand Hessians soon threw down their arms. Only a troop of light horse made its escape towards Princeton.

As Washington knew that he could not hold Trenton against the force which would be hurried there in a few hours, he recrossed the Delaware with his prisoners and spoils. He had lost only four men, two of whom had been frozen. He had captured twelve hundred fine muskets, six brass cannon, and all the flags and standards of the brigade. Most important, perhaps, the patriots gained much needed food supplies.

This brilliant victory filled the despondent patriots with joy and the British with amazement. General Howe, who was taking his ease in winter quarters at New York, in great alarm ordered Lord Cornwallis back to Princeton to reinforce General Grant.

Congress now gave Washington absolute control of the war. "Happy is the country," wrote the committee, "when the general of their forces can be entrusted with the most unlimited power."

About 1400 veteran soldiers whose terms were about to expire were induced by Washington to remain six weeks longer. With the return of victory to the Americans, many supporters of the English crown (Tories) in the Jerseys declared themselves patriots and began to enlist. The ray of hope began to gleam once more between the clouds of adversity. So closed the year of our Lord and of American Independence, 1776.

CHAPTER EIGHT

The Days of War

Four days after the capture of the Hessians, Washington, with four thousand men, again crossed the Delaware through the floating ice and halted at Trenton. It was almost madness to venture within the grasp of Lord Cornwallis, who had moved forward so rapidly that by Jan. 1, 1777, he was in front of Washington with seven thousand men. The American officers, however, felt that another effort should be made to defeat the enemy and save Philadelphia before General Howe could come up with reinforcements.

New Jersey Campaigns
1776 - 1777

Washington's route ─ ─ ─ ─→

0   5   10   15 MILES

A sharp skirmish took place outside of Trenton on the evening of the first of January. Washington then deemed it more prudent to withdraw from the town and take a stronger position behind Assunpink Creek.

The British at once took possession of the town and attempted to force the passage of the stream, but were driven back. Washington, mounted on a noble white charger, stationed himself at the south end of the stone bridge across the creek and issued his orders.

Each time the British were repulsed, loud shouts arose along the American lines.

Washington and his officers met in haste to consider their desperate situation. Only a small stream separated them from the enemy, vastly superior in numbers and discipline, while behind them flowed the Delaware filled with floating ice and impassable in the face of the foe.

In this dark hour, a bold plan was developed by Washington. The forces of the enemy were advancing by detachments from Princeton. Would it be possible by a rapid night march to pass around these forces and surprise the troops at Princeton? His officers at once agreed to the movement. The campfires were kept burning brightly throughout the night in order to deceive the enemy. About midnight, the little army was marching swiftly and silently towards Princeton, and the morning light showed the British sentries a deserted camp.

At the very moment Cornwallis found out that the camp on the Assunpink had been deserted, the Americans were entering Princeton. They met the British division beginning its march to Trenton, and the battle at once began. At first, the raw American militia gave way, but they were rallied by Washington who galloped forward and placed himself at their head. Inspired by his noble example, the men rushed forward and soon put the foe to flight, inflicting upon them a loss of four hundred and thirty men killed, wounded, and missing. The Americans lost the brave General Mercer, who, struck down by a blow from the butt of a musket, refused to surrender and was bayoneted to death. They also lost about thirty men killed and wounded.

Washington then collected his little army and pressed the enemy along the road to Brunswick, where there were valuable supplies. But his men were so fatigued by marching and fighting in a half-starved condition that he gave up the pursuit. Destroying the bridge behind him, he pushed on to the wooded heights of Morristown. There he was safe from Cornwallis, who was already marching to attack him; and he was also in position to fall upon the rear of the enemy should they proceed to Philadelphia.

Cornwallis retired to Brunswick and continued to contract his lines until all his forces were collected at that place and at Amboy.

The whole aspect of the war in the Jerseys had now changed. The people, aroused by the outrages of the Hessian and British soldiers and encouraged by the successes of Washington, openly declared themselves patriots. Congress returned to Philadelphia, and confidence was restored throughout the country. "Achievements so great," says Botta, "gained for the American commander a very great reputation. All declared him to be the savior of his country, and proclaimed him equal to the most renowned commanders of antiquity."

Meanwhile, Congress was making arrangements for carrying on the war with greater vigor. Three commissioners—Benjamin Franklin, Silas Deane, and Arthur Lee—were sent to France to borrow money from that government, and also, if possible, to prevail upon it to acknowledge the independence of the American colonies. These men excited at the court of France great interest in the American cause. Several gentlemen of rank and fortune came forward and offered their services. The most distinguished of these was the Marquis de Lafayette, a young nobleman. He fitted out a vessel at his own expense and, eluding the officers of the French ports, reached South Carolina in April, 1777. His arrival caused great joy. Washington received him as a friend, and Congress, in July of this year, commissioned him a major general.

MARQUIS DE LAFAYETTE

Congress now made a blunder which brought a train of serious consequences to the cause and to Washington. Generals Stirling, Mifflin, St. Clair, Stephens, and Lincoln were all advanced to the rank of major general while Arnold, their senior in service, who had performed so many brilliant exploits, was passed over and left a brigadier! Through the influence of Washington, Congress afterward gave Arnold the desired rank, but his haughty spirit never forgave the slight, and from that time he sought revenge.

Early in 1777, it became evident to Washington that the British were going to invade New York from Canada. For this purpose, an army of about 10,000 men under General Burgoyne was being organized. General Schuyler was in command of the American forces in eastern New York, and Washington sent him all the reinforcements that could possibly be spared.

In July 1777, General Howe with 18,000 men sailed from New York for an attack upon Philadelphia. As they were unable to ascend the Delaware River because of forts and obstructions placed near the mouth of that river by the Americans, the fleet sailed southward and, entering the Chesapeake, proceeded to Elk River in Maryland. There the troops disembarked and began to march toward Philadelphia.

Washington, who had been anxiously watching their movements, advanced to meet them. He selected the river Brandywine about 70 miles from Philadelphia as his line of defense. He knew that his poorly equipped army of 11,000 men was no match in the open field for the 18,000 British regulars; but neither the public mind nor Congress itself would have been satisfied without at least one attempt to prevent the British from entering Philadelphia.

The American commander had sent to the aid of General Schuyler several of his best regiments, among them Col. Daniel Morgan's detachment of mounted riflemen from Virginia. He now felt the need of these daring troopers, for in their absence it was difficult to find out the movements of the enemy. In

DANIEL MORGAN

doubt as to where the enemy would cross, Washington stationed the left wing of his army at a crossing on the Brandywine called Chadd's Ford, while the right, under General Sullivan, was extended for some distance up the river.

Early on the morning of September 11, the British reached the Brandywine and the battle was begun. The Hessians attacked the left wing of the Americans at the ford; but the main division of the British marched far around, by an indirect route, and crossed at a point beyond the American right. Howe had repeated his tactics of the battle of Long Island and had again outflanked the Americans. Their right wing was thrown into confusion and crushed by the attack on its rear, and the battle was lost. Washington retreated during the night to West Chester, and later on crossed the Schuylkill to Germantown.

The loss of the Americans in this battle was about 1,000 men; that of the British was 584. Major General Lafayette was severely wounded and barely escaped capture.

Finding that his men were in good spirits and that they deemed the recent affair a check rather than a defeat, Washington resolved to risk another battle in defense of the capital. On September 15, he recrossed the Schuylkill and attacked Howe's forces at Warren's Tavern. Just as the battle began, a terrific storm swept over the field. The cartridges of the combatants were soaked with rain, and fighting was impossible. Washington, therefore, withdrew his forces and retreated to a safe place on French Creek.

After a brief rest, Washington again moved forward to harass General Howe and if possible to save Philadelphia. But, after several skirmishes, Howe succeeded in evading the weary and barefooted American troops, and by a forced march threw his forces across the river. On September 26, 1777, the splendidly arrayed British army entered the city, stepping proudly to the music of "God save the King." The Tories were wild with joy, and the British regarded the taking of the capital as the end of the war.

But they did not reckon upon the wisdom and patience of the "American Fabius" who, undismayed, advanced toward Germantown, where the main division of the British was quartered. On October 4, Washington attempted to surprise this force, but owing to the roughness of the roads, the attack could not be made as he had planned it. On the approach of the Americans, the British sprang to their arms and a hard fight began. In a short time, however, the enemy was forced to retreat in disorder.

In the meantime, a thick fog had arisen so dense that it was impossible to distinguish friend from foe. This fog caused a sudden and singular panic among the victorious Americans. In the darkness, Wayne's division, which had driven a part of the enemy's forces several miles from their camp, became alarmed by the advance of a large body of troops upon its rear. Imagining that they were being surrounded by the British, his men fell back in confusion upon the supporting columns, which in turn retreated. Then, in spite of the efforts of the officers to rally the broken ranks, our army fled in the moment of victory.

Finding that they were not being pursued, the British recovered from their surprise and rallied. About this time, the rising sun dispelled the mist and they beheld the Americans retreating in good order, carrying with them their wounded and baggage.

The Americans lost in this engagement about 1,000 killed, wounded, and missing. The total British loss was only 535. General Sullivan, in writing of this battle, says: "I saw with

great concern our brave commander in chief exposing himself to the hottest fire of the enemy in such a manner that regard for my country obliged me to ride to him and beg him to retire."

The Battle of Germantown, though a defeat for the patriots, had the effect of a victory. The boldness of the attack and the nearness of victory convinced both America and Europe that Washington was a formidable foe. With great skill and care, he now drew nearer to Philadelphia and entrenched his army at White Marsh. In this position he was able to cut off many supplies intended for the British.

To save their army from starvation, General Howe now resolved to destroy Fort Mifflin and Fort Mercer, which commanded the Delaware River below Philadelphia and prevented the entrance of the British fleet. After a fierce bombardment, both forts were captured. By November 20, General Howe had at last obtained full control of the Delaware River.

While these movements had been going on around Philadelphia, the American army under General Gates, who had superseded General Schuyler, had captured at Saratoga, New York, on October 17, the entire British army under General Burgoyne. The victory, which was largely due to the bravery and daring of Arnold, gained for the Americans a fine train of artillery, seven thousand stands of arms, military stores of all kinds, and undisputed possession of the eastern part of the state of New York.

The recent victory at Saratoga under Generals Gates and Arnold had rendered the public impatient for something equally brilliant from the army of the commander in chief. Great pressure was now brought to bear upon Washington to attempt the storming of Philadelphia. But knowing the strength of the British fortifications, he refused to risk his army for the satisfaction of the public and the favor of the press.

About this time, arrangements were made by Howe to surprise Washington in his camp at White Marsh. The plan was revealed to the commander by Mrs. Darrah, a Quaker lady, at whose house Howe had held a council of war. When the British approached the American camp, they found the patriots in order of battle. So complete were the preparations for defense that Howe did not dare attack.

Winter now set in with great severity, and Washington sought winter quarters for his army at a place called Valley Forge, twenty-two miles from Philadelphia. From this place, he could watch that city and also protect a large extent of country from the ravages of the British.

A town of log huts was soon built and Washington strove by every means possible to secure needed supplies for his suffering men. The colonies had not sent the promised supplies to their soldiers, and Congress was unable to buy provisions with its worthless paper money. Food was scarce and thousands of soldiers had no shoes. Many were without winter clothes, and even straw was unavailable to raise them at night from the cold, wet earth. Disease attacked them, and the hospitals were filled as fast as the dead were carried out. The pay of the officers was not sufficient to buy food and clothing, and many of the bravest and best resigned.

Amidst the griefs and cares to which Washington was subjected, a plot was formed to have Congress remove him and place General Gates at the head of the army. These were perhaps the darkest days of Washington's life. But he paid no attention to the malice of his private enemies. Calm and resolute, he bent all of his energies to improve the condition of his army and camp. When at last the news of the plot to remove him spread abroad throughout the land, the people took his side, and the army was so indignant that all who had aided in the foul conspiracy were so afraid of its righteous anger that they kept out of camp.

After much delay on the part of Congress, Baron Steuben was appointed inspector general of the army, and General Greene, quartermaster general. Under the supervision of these officers the condition of affairs at Valley Forge improved wonderfully. The soldiers were regularly and carefully drilled by the inspector general, and the arrival of provisions and supplies of all kinds as the result of the efforts of the quartermaster general removed the dread of famine from the hearts of the heroic band.

Washington was a great man, not only in big things, but in little things. He was never too great to do a kindness. He was never too high to stoop to those who were lower than he and in need of help. There was one rule which he tried always to obey. It was this: "Make sure you are doing what is right with God—then do it with all your strength."

One day, when his army was in camp, Washington walked out alone to enjoy the morning air and see what was happening. As it was winter, he had put on a long overcoat that hid his uniform; and so many of the soldiers among whom he passed did not know that he was the general.

At one place, there was a young corporal with his men building a small fort made of logs. They were about to lift a very heavy log when Washington came up.

"Heave ho!" cried the little corporal. "Up with it, men! Up with it!" But he did not lift a hand to help his men. The young men lifted with all their might. The log was almost in its place, but it was so heavy they could not move it any further.

The corporal cried again, "Heave ho! Up with it!" The young soldiers could not lift it more; their strength was almost gone, and the log was about to fall.

Then Washington ran up, and with his strong arms gave them the help they so much needed. The big log was lifted upon the fort, and the men gave their thanks to the tall stranger who had been so kind. But the corporal said nothing.

"Why don't you take hold and help your men with this heavy lifting?" asked Washington.

"Why don't I?" said the little man. "Don't you see that I am the corporal?"

"Oh, indeed!" said Washington, as he unbuttoned his overcoat and showed the uniform which he wore. "Well, I am the general; and the next time you have a log too heavy for your men to lift, send for me."

You can imagine how the little corporal felt when he saw that it was General Washington who stood before him. It was a good lesson for him, and there are still little men living today who could learn a good lesson from this story. We find the source of this lesson in the Holy Bible, for it teaches that "And whoever will be chief among you, let him be your servant" (Matthew 20:27).

On February 6, 1778, a treaty of defensive alliance was concluded between France and the United States. The king of France acknowledged the independence of the United States and sent money, supplies, and a fleet to aid the Americans.

Great was the rejoicing throughout the colonies, for all felt that with so powerful an ally the British would at last be defeated. The treaty was celebrated at Valley Forge with solemn thanksgiving by a chaplain at the head of each brigade, a grand parade, and a national salute of thirteen guns. A banquet followed, at which Washington dined in public with all his officers. Upon his return from the banquet, he was greeted with the wildest applause from both officers and men. A renewed sense of hope and confidence began to grow in the hearts of those stationed at Valley Forge.

One day, while camped at Valley Forge, a Tory who was well known in the neighborhood was captured and brought into camp. His name was Michael Wittman, and he was accused of having carried aid and information to the British in Philadelphia. He was taken to West Chester and there tried by court-martial. It was proved that he was a very dangerous man and that he had more than once attempted to do great harm to the American army. He was pronounced guilty of being a spy and sentenced to be hanged.

On the evening of the day before that set for the execution, a strange old man appeared at Valley Forge. He was a small man with long, snow-white hair falling over his shoulders. His face, although full of kindliness, was sad-looking and thoughtful; his eyes, which were bright and sharp, were upon the ground and lifted only when he was speaking.

His name was announced, and Washington immediately recognized this visitor as an old friend.

"Peter Miller?" said Washington. "Certainly, show him in at once."

"General Washington, I have come to ask a great favor of you," he said, in his usual kindly tones.

"I shall be glad to grant you almost anything," said Washington, "for we surely are indebted to you for many favors. Tell me what it is."

"I hear," said Peter, "that Michael Wittman has been found guilty of treason and that he is to be hanged at Turk's Head tomorrow. I have come to ask you to pardon him."

Washington started back, and a cloud came over his face.

"That is impossible," he said. "Wittman is a bad man. He has done all in his power to betray us. He has even offered to join the British and aid in destroying us. In these times, we dare not be lenient with traitors; and for that reason I cannot pardon your friend."

"Friend!" cried Peter. "Why, he is no friend of mine. He is my bitterest enemy. He has persecuted me for years. He has even beaten me and spit in my face, knowing full well that I would not strike back. Michael Wittman is no friend of mine."

Washington was puzzled. "And still you wish me to pardon him?" he asked.

"I do," answered Peter. "I ask it of you as a great personal favor."

"Tell me," said Washington, with hesitating voice, "why is it that you thus ask the pardon of your worst enemy?"

"I ask it because Jesus did as much for me," was the old man's brief answer.

Washington turned away and went into another room. Soon he returned with a paper on which was written the pardon of Michael Wittman.

"My dear friend," he said, as he placed it in the old man's hands, "I thank you for this example of Christian charity."

While waiting at Valley Forge, news of the sailing of the French fleet so alarmed the British government that orders were sent to the army at Philadelphia to join the forces at New York. General Howe, at his own request, had been recalled to England, and Sir Henry Clinton had been put in command at Philadelphia. On June 18, 1778, he evacuated the city and began to make his way across the Jerseys.

Washington at once marched into the capital and then followed the retiring British. He came up with them at Monmouth on June 27. The following morning, General Charles Lee, who had been recently exchanged for the British general, Prescott, was ordered to commence the attack with five thousand men. Washington promised to come to his assistance with the main army.

The British turned to meet the attack of the Americans. Surprised at the determination of Clinton to give battle with his whole army, Lee was forced to form his troops upon unfavorable ground. Behind him was a morass over which it would have been difficult to retreat in case of defeat. It has been suggested that he was angry at being forced to an engagement which he had opposed in the council of war held previously by Washington. However that may be, instead of advancing, at the first charge of the British he ordered a retreat; and his men ran pellmell across the morass, followed by the enemy.

In the meantime, Washington, ignorant of the shameful retreat, was coming up with the other divisions of the army. As the first sound of firing burst upon the air, his troops eager for battle, threw aside their knapsacks and pressed forward. The heat was so intense and the dust and sand so deep in the roads that many fell exhausted upon the way.

Washington had dismounted and was standing with his arm thrown across the neck of his snow-white charger listening to the firing in front and watching his men as they marched past to battle, when a farmer dashed up to him and exclaimed that Lee's division was in full retreat and near at hand.

With one terrible look of anger and despair, Washington mounted his horse and galloped swiftly to meet the retreating men. The moment that he was seen, a ringing shout, "Long live Washington," burst upon his ears. Galloping to the rear, he reined up beside Lee and in a voice full of passion said, "General Lee, I desire to know what is the reason, and whence this disorder and confusion." Greatly disconcerted, Lee stammered a reply, but Washington galloped on, ordering the officers and encouraging the men until they wheeled and formed in splendid order to meet the approaching foe.

He then rode back to Lee and, pointing to the line of battle, said, "Will you, sir, command in that place?"

He replied, "Yes."

"Well, then," said Washington, "I expect you to check the enemy at once."

"Your orders shall be obeyed," replied Lee, "and I shall not be the first to leave the field." He immediately put himself at the head of the columns, while Washington returned to lead up the second division. But Lee found it impossible to remedy his fatal mistake. Both he and his men fought bravely, but they were gradually pressed back by the British. Washington then came up rapidly with troops under Wayne and Greene, and by nightfall the British had been driven back across the morass to the high ground beyond. Darkness now came on and the battle ceased.

Although worn out by the excessive heat and fatigue of battle, the Americans slept upon their arms so that they might attack the enemy at early dawn. Washington, having visited his outposts, lay down beneath a tree with Lafayette by his side. But when morning came, they found that Sir Henry Clinton had quietly withdrawn during the night to the heights of Middletown.

The loss of the Americans in the Battle of Monmouth was 227; that of the enemy was much greater.

The British forces pursued their way to New York. Washington followed them and, crossing the Hudson, once more took up his quarters at White Plains.

On the day after the Battle of Monmouth, Washington received an insulting letter from Lee demanding an apology for his hasty words on the field of battle. Washington replied severely that his language on the previous day had been warranted by the circumstances and that he had no apology to make. Lee answered in a still more insulting manner, and was thereupon arrested. He was tried by court-martial and dismissed from the army for twelve months. He then retired to his estate in Virginia and never more entered the service.

On July 11, 1778, the French fleet under Count D'Estaing arrived. It was his intention to attack the British squadron in New York Harbor; but as the large warships of the line could not cross the bar, the plan was abandoned. The fleet then sailed to Newport, R.I., where the British had established themselves in force.

Washington had sent to Newport General Sullivan and Marquis de Lafayette with two brigades to cooperate with the French fleet. Quartermaster general Greene was also ordered there, as he was a native of the island on which Newport is situated and was well acquainted with its shores and people.

Before operations had fully commenced, Admiral Lord Howe appeared with a part of his squadron. D'Estaing sailed forth to meet the enemy, but a terrific storm separated the combatants. Howe made for New York and the French fleet returned to Newport, battered and crippled by the storm. D'Estaing now refused to assist General Sullivan, so the latter had to stop his siege and retreat, which he did in a masterly manner.

The failure of this expedition was a great disappointment to Washington; for the country expected much from the cooperation of the French, and was bitter in its denunciation of D'Estaing.

Before the winter had begun, Washington distributed his troops in a line of strong encampments from Long Island Sound to the Delaware. In this way, the country was better protected and the troops were made more comfortable. Sir Henry Clinton still kept possession of New York and contented himself with sending out expeditions for the purpose of plundering the countryside.

Washington now lost the assistance and companionship of the generous Lafayette. Seeing no prospect of immediate warfare, Lafayette obtained a furlough from Congress and returned to France, promising to come back to America, "... whenever he should find it convenient."

Much of the commander in chief's time this winter was passed in Philadelphia planning for the campaign of 1779.

CHAPTER NINE

Victory at Last

When the spring of 1779 opened, Sir Henry Clinton sent an expedition up the Hudson and took possession of Stony Point and Verplanck Point, the lower gates to the Highlands. On June 1, Governor Tryon made a sudden descent on New Haven, Connecticut, and compelled a surrender. Several towns were burned to ashes and quantities of plunder were carried off. Norfolk and other towns in Virginia were burned.

These raids caused Washington much vexation, though, of course, with his small army it was impossible for him to meet every attack of the British, who moved up and down the coast with their powerful squadrons.

It was very important, however, to the Americans that Stony Point should be retaken. Washington at last decided to entrust the task to General Wayne, "Mad Anthony" as he was sometimes called. That brave officer marched against the fort and in the evening of July 15, 1779, halted his force of one thousand men in the woods nearby.

From this point, they were guided by a citizen named Pompey, who knew the British countersign. The pickets were surprised and gagged in the darkness. The muskets of the Americans were then unloaded and the bayonets fixed in utter silence. At midnight, the patriots charged and scaled the ramparts. The British, finding themselves between two lines of glittering steel, surrendered.

General Wayne secured the ammunition and supplies, destroyed the fort, and marched off with more than five hundred prisoners. This was one of the most brilliant victories in the War for American Independence.

About a month later, the heart of Washington was cheered by another victory. Major Henry Lee, of the Virginia Dragoons, in the course of his scouting, had discovered that the British post at Paulus Hook (Jersey City) just opposite New York City, was very negligently guarded. He proposed to take this fort by surprise and Washington gave his permission. Favored by the darkness of the night, Lee, with about five hundred men, surprised the fort within gunshot of New York and carried off its garrison of one hundred and fifty-nine men.

Washington now established his headquarters at West Point, the mountain fortress on the Hudson, where he superintended in person the fortifications of the Highlands. Here he received the news that Count D'Estaing, with a powerful fleet, after having made a successful cruise against the English in the West Indies, had arrived off the coast of Georgia. He hoped that the Count would sail north and that they could arrange to make a combined attempt to take New York City. But D'Estaing was persuaded to assist General Lincoln, who was now in command of the Southern army, to retake Savannah from the British. The attempt, however, failed through the obstinacy of the French admiral.

Seeing that no reliance could be placed upon D'Estaing's cooperation, Washington sent the militia and Southern troops home and prepared for the winter of 1779–1780. The war this year had progressed very slowly and the patriotism of the people seemed to grow cold.

One division of the army was left at West Point; the other, under Washington, wintered in huts along the heights of Morristown. This winter was but a repetition of that at Valley Forge. The weather was unusually severe. The commissaries had neither money nor credit with which to purchase supplies for the suffering men. The beginning of the year 1780 found the army facing starvation. "For a fortnight past," wrote Washington, "the troops, both officers and men, have been almost perishing with hunger. Yet they have borne their sufferings with a patience that merits the approbation, and ought to excite the sympathy, of their countrymen."

The depreciation of the paper currency was the chief cause of trouble. Forty dollars in paper was worth only one in gold or silver. The pay of a colonel would not buy a bushel of oats for his horse, and four months' pay of a private soldier would not provide his family with one bushel of wheat. In this emergency, Congress promised to make good to the troops the difference in the value of their pay caused by this depreciation.

Washington was compelled to obtain grain and cattle by calling upon the counties of New Jersey for supplies. Whenever the call was unheeded, the articles required were impressed—that is, taken by force. In this way, the army was kept from dissolution and starvation.

In this gloomy time, a letter came to Washington from Lafayette announcing his arrival at Boston. We are told that tears came into Washington's eyes as he read this most welcome letter, telling that his friend was coming and that help was at hand; for Lafayette brought the news that another French fleet and an army under Count Rochambeau would soon come to the assistance of the Americans.

Washington's attention was now drawn to affairs in the South. Leaving a large body of men at New York, in January, Sir Henry Clinton sailed south and moved upon Charleston. After a brave resistance, General Lincoln was forced to surrender the city with about 2,000 troops.

This was a sad time for the patriots. Georgia and South Carolina were overrun by the British, the money troubles were growing worse, and two regiments from Connecticut had mutinied in Washington's camp. He again appealed to Congress for prompt assistance. But having no credit, Congress could not procure even provisions for the famishing army. In the midst of this distress, Robert Morris and a few other wealthy patriots came forward with their private fortunes and saved the country from impending ruin.

About this time, the patriotic women of Philadelphia, headed by Mrs. Washington, sent about seven thousand dollars to Washington to spend as he thought best for his men. Everywhere, but chiefly in the Carolinas, the women now rekindled the fires of patriotism which had burned so brightly in the beginning of the Revolution. Their parting plea to husband and lover was, "Prefer prisons to infamy and death to servitude." In other words, the noble women of the land reminded the nation of the immortal words of Patrick Henry; "… Give me liberty or give me death!"

Sir Henry Clinton, after capturing Charleston, had overrun the whole state of South Carolina. He left Lord Cornwallis and Lord Rowdon to hold the conquered territory and returned to New York, landing on June 17, 1780. But almost immediately his troops embarked again, as if for an expedition up the Hudson.

Fearing for the safety of West Point, Washington set off towards that place, leaving General Greene to protect the stores and camp at Morristown. As soon as his departure was reported to Sir Henry Clinton, he sent a large body of infantry and cavalry to capture Morristown. But General Greene had so posted his little force in the mountain passes that the British troops were beaten back and forced to retreat in haste, pursued and harassed by the American dragoons and the militia of the country. The next morning, the British crossed over to Staten Island, and New Jersey was at last freed from their presence.

Keeping a strict watch upon the Highlands of the Hudson, Washington turned his attention to the army of the South. He decided to send General Greene to assume command in place of General Lincoln who had been captured. But Congress, with undue haste and without consulting Washington,

GENERAL GATES

gave General Gates, the conqueror of Burgoyne, that important command.

In the meantime, the insolence of the British troops had aroused the people of the Carolinas. They flocked to the standards of Marion and Sumter, who now came forward as protectors of the cause of liberty. They kept their headquarters in thick swamps, from which they would suddenly spring by night or day and attack the enemy with such fury as to sweep all before them. During the whole summer and autumn of 1780, Colonel Marion continued to sweep around Cornwallis's encampments, cutting his lines of communication and keeping him in a constant state of uneasiness. The British soon nicknamed Colonel Marion the "swamp fox" and offered a reward for his capture, dead or alive.

Early in August, Washington directed General Gates, who had now collected his forces, to advance to meet Cornwallis. The hostile armies, each making an attempt to surprise the other, met near Camden in the darkness of the night. By mutual consent they waited for the dawn before beginning the fight. The Americans were defeated with a loss of more than 1,000 men, among whom was the brave Baron de Kalb. General Gates was recalled and General Greene was placed in command of the scattered and disheartened patriot army.

We have now arrived at one of the saddest episodes of the struggle for independence, and one which gave the keenest anguish to our revered commander in chief—the treason of Benedict Arnold.

Having received a severe wound at the Battle of Saratoga in the fall of 1777, Arnold had been made commandant of Philadelphia. While living there, he married Miss Shippen, the beautiful daughter of a wealthy Tory residing in that city.

He soon began to live a lifestyle of extravagance that quickly over-whelmed him with debt.

In order to obtain money, he made false entries in his accounts with the government. When they were discovered, eight charges were pre-ferred against him by Congress, and he was convicted by a court-martial and sentenced to be reprimanded by Washington. Believing that Arnold had been badly treated, Washing-

BENEDICT ARNOLD

ton performed his task as gently as possible; but Arnold was deeply mortified and enraged. Pressed down by his debts and burning for revenge, he entered into a secret correspondence with Sir Henry Clinton, at New York, and finally agreed to betray his country for British gold.

Disguising his real feelings and professing unaltered devo-tion to his country, he applied for the command of West Point, the key to the Highlands of the Hudson. As Washington knew his great merit as an officer and did not doubt his patriotism, he was placed in command of that important fortress.

Arnold was now in a position not only to demand from Sir Henry a reward for betraying his country but also to satisfy his desire for revenge. At last, it was secretly agreed that the British fleet should ascend the Hudson and that the garrison and fortress of West Point should be surrendered without a struggle.

Clinton, who believed that the loss of this fort would put an end to "the rebellion," sent Major John André, his adju-tant general, to confer with the traitor on the terms of the surrender. André sailed up the Hudson on board the *Vulture*, a British sloop-of-war, and landed on the evening of July 21 a few miles below West Point. Shortly after midnight, he was met by Arnold in a thicket near the shore. Here their plans were discussed until daylight compelled them to withdraw to a house within the American lines. André, being in full

British uniform, was now obliged to disguise himself, and by so doing he assumed the character of a spy.

The day was spent by Arnold and André in completing the bargain. Arnold agreed to surrender West Point for ten thousand pounds and a commission as brigadier general in the British army. André received from Arnold papers containing plans of West Point and a statement of its condition, which he concealed in his stockings.

In the meantime, the *Vulture*, lying at anchor in the Hudson, had been discovered by some American gunners, who fired their cannons and drove it down the river. This forced André to set out for New York on foot. Crossing the river, he passed the American outposts in safety, bearing Arnold's passport and giving the name of John Anderson.

Near Tarrytown, almost within sight of the British lines, he was stopped by three patriots, John Paulding, David Williams, and Isaac Van Wort. Supposing that they were Tories, André confessed himself a British officer; but on discovering his mistake, he produced Arnold's pass and begged that he might continue his journey. But as the suspicions of the patriots had been aroused, they searched him and found the papers in his stockings. They delivered him to Colonel Jameson at Northcastle, who at once notified Arnold that "John Anderson" had been taken with his passport and some papers relating to West Point.

Arnold was at breakfast when Jameson's letter was handed to him. He sprang up from the table, exchanged a few hurried words with his wife, and fled to the river. He succeeded in reaching the *Vulture* in a small boat.

Washington, attended by General Lafayette and General Knox, reached Arnold's headquarters shortly after the traitor's flight. When Washington was informed of the deep-laid treachery, he was at first quiet and amazed. But, recovering his usual calmness, he at once began the work of strengthening the garrison and completing the works about the fortress; for none knew so well as Arnold its weak places. Though outwardly calm, Washington's trust in those around him was greatly shaken. He said privately to Lafayette and Knox, in tones of great distress, "Whom can we trust now?"

Arnold had escaped, but André was left to his fate. He was tried by a court-martial and condemned to death as a spy. Sir Henry Clinton made every effort to save his favorite aide, but in vain. On October 2, 1780, he was led to the scaffold and hanged. Arnold, safe with the British, received the payment agreed upon for his treachery, and afterward, as we shall see, inflicted great injuries upon his native country.

The year 1781 opened ingloriously for the patriot cause. The army was again without food, pay, or proper clothing. Its condition was so desperate that the Pennsylvania troops broke from their barracks on New Year's Day and marched on Philadelphia. They were met by commissioners of Congress who promised to fulfill all their demands. Knowing how shamefully his men had been treated, Washington was not unwilling that Congress should reap the reward of its neglect. Not long after, a New Jersey brigade revolted. This movement Washington thought necessary to punish. The men were overpowered and subjected to severe discipline. After this, the army was no more troubled by mutiny.

Early in January, Arnold, now a British officer, was sent with an army to devastate southern Virginia. Having desolated the banks of the James, he landed near Richmond and succeeded in burning and destroying a large amount of public and private property in that city and vicinity. One of the plundering expeditions reached Mount Vernon and would have burned it had not the manager of the place ransomed it by bringing out large quantities of forage and provisions. When Washington heard of this, he was much displeased, and wrote that he would have been less vexed to hear that his home was in ruins than that he had furnished aid to the enemy.

As soon as Washington found out that active warfare was being waged in Virginia, he sent Lafayette with a force of twelve hundred men to defend that colony. Virginia was at this time helpless, as most of her fighting men were absent in Greene's and Washington's armies.

In the meantime, Cornwallis had arrived from North Carolina and taken charge of the campaign in Virginia. After capturing Richmond, he began to plunder and pillage the country north of the James River.

As the young general named Lafayette had too small a force to meet Cornwallis in the field, he skillfully eluded him until reinforced by General Wayne with about nine hundred Pennsylvania troops. He then changed his tactics and assumed an aggressive posture. On the approach of the forces under Lafayette, Cornwallis moved eastward towards Williamsburg, followed and harassed by the Americans. After a stay of nine days there, he moved to Portsmouth.

According to orders from Sir Henry Clinton, Cornwallis, in the early part of August, moved his army from Portsmouth to Yorktown on the York River a few miles from its entrance into the Chesapeake. The York River is here about one mile wide and deep enough for the largest ships to ride at anchor.

Lafayette, supported by General Wayne, quickly moved his little army into the peninsula between the York and the James rivers and took his position only eight miles from the enemy. A powerful French fleet under Count De Grasse was soon expected in the Chesapeake, and Lafayette saw at a glance that if the York River could be blockaded by a friendly fleet, and a sufficient land force be brought to bear upon Yorktown, Cornwallis would be forced to surrender.

To carry out this plan, Washington determined to leave a small force to guard the Hudson and to proceed to Virginia with the American and French troops. He took the precaution to mislead Sir Henry Clinton by making him believe that an assault was about to be directed against New York. His forces were pressed as closely as possible to the city. So well were his plans laid that Clinton did not know that Washington was marching south until he had reached the Delaware. It was then too late for him to give chase.

In order to divert Washington, Sir Henry sent Arnold to devastate New London, Connecticut, his native place. This he did in a most horrible manner. But Washington did not change his plans, knowing full well that it was critically important to capture Cornwallis. As Washington marched through Philadelphia, he procured through Mr. Robert Morris twenty thousand dollars in silver to pay off some of the northern regiments that objected to going south. This amount was really furnished by Count Rochambeau and was repaid in October with money given to the American cause by the king of France.

On the way southward, Washington stayed two days at Mount Vernon. It had been six long years of toil and anxiety since he had slept under the beloved roof of his home. Count Rochambeau and other French officers joined him there and were entertained in true old Virginia style.

At Williamsburg, he was met by Lafayette, who reported that Count De Grasse had entered the Chesapeake with twenty-eight ships of the line with nearly four thousand infantry, and was already blockading the mouth of the York River. At last, Washington had obtained the cooperation of the land and naval forces. On September 28, the allied armies encamped closely around Yorktown and the siege was officially begun.

Up to this time, Cornwallis had felt very secure, being sure that he could not be hurt by Lafayette, whom he referred to as "the boy." But when he found himself surrounded both by land and water, he began to build fortifications; he also sent off messengers to Sir Henry Clinton to inform him of the situation.

About October 1, the Americans threw up two redoubts or bunkers, which were severely pounded by cannon. We are told that while Washington was superintending their defense, a shot struck the ground nearby, covering him with dust. The Rev. Mr. Evans, chaplain in the army, was greatly frightened. Taking off his hat, he found it covered with sand. "See here, General!" said he in an excited manner.

Movement from Newport and New York to Yorktown

"Mr. Evans," said Washington, with subtle humor, "you had better carry that hat home and show it to your wife and children."

"When the batteries of the first line of entrenchments were ready to fire upon the town," says an eyewitness, "Washington put the first match to the gun, and a furious cannonade commenced along the American line." After this firing had been continued for several days, Washington decided to make a night assault on two advanced redoubts held by the British.

The American detachment, commanded by Lafayette and headed by Alexander Hamilton, aide to Washington, led the attack on the right; the French attacked the left. The Americans, relying upon their bayonets, rushed forward with unloaded guns and quickly took the redoubt. The French, on their side, proceeded more scientifically; but at length, animated by their leaders, they carried the enemy's works with the bayonet. Cornwallis made no effort to retake the redoubts and they were included in a second line of entrenchments, which the allies completed before dawn.

Cornwallis now foresaw that when the besiegers should open fire upon him from their new works there would be no hope of escape. The greater part of his artillery had been thrown down, and his fortifications were in ruins. Nevertheless, he ordered a night assault. His soldiers made a brave but unsuccessful attempt to drive the allies from their advanced position. He then attempted to escape by crossing the river and trying his fate upon the opposite shore. But a terrible storm arose and the attempt was futile. The very elements seemed to unite their strength with that of the allied armies. Seeing no hope of aid, Cornwallis sent a flag of truce to Washington, and the terms of surrender were very soon agreed upon.

At two o'clock on the afternoon of October 19, 1781, Major General O'Hara led out the whole British army from the trenches into the open field, where in the presence of the allied ranks of America and France, seven thousand two hundred and forty-seven English and Hessian soldiers laid down their arms and became prisoners of war. Lord Cornwallis did not appear, but sent his sword by General O'Hara. As a solace for the mortification he had felt at the surrender of Charleston the year before, General Lincoln was selected by Washington to receive Cornwallis's sword. General Washington would only receive the sword of surrender personally if it were offered to him by Cornwallis himself.

The conquered were treated with great kindness by their conquerors. Lord Cornwallis, however, felt deeply his great misfortune. It is said that on one occasion, when he was standing before Washington with his hat off, the latter remarked, "My lord, you had better be covered from the cold."

"It matters not, sir," replied Cornwallis, raising his hand to his brow, "it matters not what becomes of this head now."

On the morning after the surrender, Washington issued a general order congratulating the allied armies on their recent victory. He also celebrated the event by releasing all who were under military arrest and by ordering divine services to be held throughout the camp in recognition of the help provided by Almighty God.

News of this important victory spread rapidly through the country. One of Washington's aides, young Tench Tilghman, carried the glad tidings to Congress at Philadelphia. When the sentinels of the city called the hour of ten o'clock on the night of his arrival they shouted, "Ten o'clock, starlight night, and Cornwallis is taken." The next morning, Congress joyfully assembled and voted thanks to the commander in chief, to Rochambeau and De Grasse, and to the officers and men of both armies.

The surrendered army of Cornwallis was marched under guard to Lancaster, Pennsylvania, there to await a prisoner exchange; and the American army went into camp once more on the Hudson and in New Jersey. The French army wintered in Virginia with headquarters at Williamsburg.

Having attended to all the arrangements for the comfort of both armies, Washington left Yorktown and hurried to Eltham, the home of his friend Colonel Barrett. Here his beloved stepson, John Parke Custis, was lying very ill. Only a short while after his arrival, the young man breathed his last. As a consolation to Mrs. Washington, the general adopted the two youngest of the children, George Washington Parke Custis and Eleanor, better known as "Nellie Custis."

The surrender at Yorktown was really the end of the war, though the treaty of peace made at Paris was not signed until February 1783. Until peace had been concluded, Washington remained with the army, keeping it intact and preventing quarrels and discontent among the officers and men. Writing of the discontent that prevailed in the spring of 1782 in the camp at Newburg, an eminent historian says, "Nothing but their love of Washington restrained the army from asserting their rights by violence; and never did Washington display more judgment than in dealing with his poor, unpaid soldiers at this critical moment."

In May 1782, Washington received a letter from Colonel Nicola, through whom the troops generally made their complaints, setting forth the belief of the army that Congress would never redress their wrongs, and begging that Washington would allow them to place him as king at the head of the nation. Filled with grief and alarm, Washington rejected the offer and told them that "the reestablishment of royalty would be fatal to those liberties which were more precious than life."

On November 25, 1783, the last of the British left New York, and on the next day the Americans marched in. General Washington and Governor Clinton, with their attendants, rode at the head of the procession.

A few days previous to this, the army had been disbanded by order of Congress. At Washington's request, the men were permitted to take with them the arms with which they had fought. He issued a touching farewell address to his soldiers, and after the departure of the British he spoke to his officers one final time. During his farewell address to the army, he was quick to observe how improbable was their hope of victory apart from a miracle of Divine grace. He remarked:

> The singular interpositions of Providence in our feeble condition were such, as could scarcely escape the attention of the most unobserving; while the unparalleled perseverance of the armies of the United States, through almost every possible suffering and discouragement for the space of eight long years, was little short of a standing miracle.

"Washington's farewell to his officers was," says the historian Headly, "an affecting scene. There were Greene and Knox and Stueben and Hamilton and others who had stood shoulder to shoulder in the deadly fray, and who with equal courage had faced disaster and famine. All that they had undergone together rushed into their minds."

Standing in the midst of them, Washington said slowly: "With a heart full of love and gratitude, I now take leave of you, most devoutly wishing that your latter days may be as prosperous and happy as your former ones have been glorious and honorable." He then added with emotion: "I cannot come to each of you to take my leave, but shall be obliged if each of you will come and take me by the hand."

General Knox was nearest and was the first to advance. Washington grasped his hand and clasped him in his arms. Their emotions were too deep for utterance—not a word was spoken. The others followed. Then in silence their beloved commander preceded them from the room. Escorted by a corps of light infantry, they walked slowly to Whitehall Ferry. Having entered the barge, Washington turned to them, took off his hat, and waved a silent farewell.

On his way to Annapolis, Washington stopped in Philadelphia and adjusted with the comptroller of the treasury his accounts from the commencement of the war. The total amount was about fourteen thousand five hundred pounds sterling, every item being entered by his own hand. This sum had actually been expended by him during the war from his own purse. It must be remembered that he would receive no pay for his own services. "This account," says one of his biographers, "stands a touchstone of honesty in office and a lasting rebuke on that lavish expenditure of the public money too often indulged in by military commanders."

Having arrived at Annapolis, it was determined that at twelve o'clock on December 23, 1783, he would offer to Congress his resignation. At that hour, the gallery and a greater part of the floor of the hall of Congress were filled with ladies, members of Congress, and general officers.

"Washington entered," says Irving, "conducted by the secretary of Congress, and took a seat in a chair prepared for him. After a brief pause, the president, General Mifflin, informed him that the United States in Congress assembled were prepared to receive his communication."

Washington then arose and, while a silence like that of death filled the chamber, made a brief speech concluding thus: "Having now finished the work assigned me, I retire from the great theater of action, and bidding an affectionate farewell to this august body, under whose orders I have so long acted, I here offer my commission and take my leave of all the employments of public life." He then advanced and laid his commission in the president's hand.

General Mifflin replied in a most touching manner, offering the commander in chief the homage of a grateful nation and invoking upon him the blessing of the Almighty.

Seldom has such a sight been seen—a victorious commander, with royalty within his reach, gladly resigning his power and retiring to private life.

CHAPTER TEN

The Citizen and President

Upon leaving Annapolis, Washington hastened toward his estate at Mount Vernon, where he arrived on Christmas eve in time for the festivities of that joyous season celebrating the Savior's birth. For some weeks, he was kept at home by the ice and snow of an unusually severe winter; but from letters written at that time, we discover how much he enjoyed the repose of domestic life and the comforts of his old home.

It was not long before he became deeply interested in looking over accounts and in adjusting his long neglected private affairs. In the midst of these labors, he received from Congress an offer of a gift of money as a reward for his distinguished services. This gift he firmly but respectfully refused. He was in need just then of cash money, for his financial affairs had suffered much during his long absences from home; but no persuasions could induce him to take pay for services rendered to his country.

When spring returned, visitors began to frequent Mount Vernon. They were received by Washington and his wife with simple and cordial hospitality. "Mrs. Washington," says a noted writer, "had a cheerful good sense that always made her an agreeable companion, and she was also an excellent manager. She, who had presided with quiet dignity at headquarters and cheered the wintry gloom of Valley Forge with her presence, presided over her duties at Mount Vernon with grace."

Washington's thoughts, however, soon turned to the region of the Ohio, the scene of his early toils and disasters whence he had written his first letter to his betrothed wife, Mrs. Custis. Again we see him accompanied by his old friend

Dr. Craik, wending his way slowly across the mountains over which he had "spurred in the days of his youthful vigor."

The object of this journey was to survey his lands on the Monongahela and Great Kanawha rivers, and to examine the routes across the mountains and along the headwaters of the Potomac and Ohio rivers. Upon reaching the Monongahela, he heard such rumors of trouble among the Indians of the Kanawha Valley that he concluded not to venture among them. So he turned his attention to "the practicability of making a short and easy connection between the Potomac and James rivers, and the waters of the Ohio, and thence on to the great chain of lakes."

This idea had taken possession of him in 1773 when he had last visited that region, but it had been put aside for the urgent duties of the War for Independence. His plan was to open up a great waterway from the lakes to the eastern ports, so that the products of the West might find their way thither instead of enriching the Spaniards of the Mississippi or the British in Canada. So enthusiastic did he become that he traveled over the proposed routes through New York, Pennsylvania, Maryland, and Virginia.

In regard to this undertaking, a well-known author says, "Among all the evidences of Washington's love of country, I consider this one of the most striking, that at that early day, without fee or reward, he should have risked his life among hostile Indians, and his health sleeping in the open woods, in countries then uninhabited. This is an act of patriotic devotion which we, at this day, can hardly believe possible."

As a result of his efforts, two companies were formed for opening the navigation of the James and the Potomac rivers. He was appointed president of both companies, and wrote at once to Mr. Jefferson, then minister to France, as to the possibility of securing a loan of money to carry out his plans. But once again he was called by the nation to more important duties. The work was completed by other hands and in other days, but Washington was the originator of the great undertaking.

In the meantime, let us see our hero at his beloved Mount Vernon. His regular life "before the war" is resumed, and he is now busily engaged in setting out shrubs and sowing seeds on the lawn. Here he is planting trees to make a denser shade, and there he is having them cut out to improve the view. He also enjoys the sports of his adopted children, George and Nellie Custis. The latter, however, in recalling her memories of him writes, "He was a silent, thoughtful man. He spoke little generally; never of himself. I never heard him relate a single act of his life during the war."

About this time, Houdon, a French artist chosen by Mr. Jefferson and Dr. Franklin, arrived at Mount Vernon to make a study of Washington for a statue ordered by the legislature of Virginia. That statue is now to be seen in the statehouse in Richmond, and is regarded as an excellent work of art.

In August 1784, Lafayette, anxious to see Washington once more, visited this country. Within a few days after landing he was at Mount Vernon in the hospitality of his beloved friend. Leaving this hospitable home, the distinguished visitor traveled through several of the states, and was received everywhere with honor and affection. When he decided to return to France in December, Washington accompanied him as far as Annapolis, and afterward wrote him a farewell letter of respect and gratitude.

Though Washington was in fact living quietly at Mount Vernon, he was watching with intense anxiety the formation of the thirteen states into a confederacy. He was in favor of a stronger but limited central government. In a letter to a friend he wrote, "I do not conceive we can exist long as a nation without lodging somewhere a power which will pervade the Union in as energetic manner as the authority of the State governments extends over its citizens."

At this time, there were many plans for establishing a better government for the new American nation, but the idea of remodeling the Articles of Confederation took form at Mount Vernon. Many of the deep thinkers of the period visited Washington and discussed with him the condition and needs of the republic, and it is positively asserted that he advised the calling of a convention to construct a more effective and efficient government. Many thoughtful minds were convinced that a new political system would have to be devised in order to prevent the country from going to ruin, although great men such as Patrick Henry feared that such changes could create a huge centralized power over the states at the expense of true liberty.

When a convention of the states was called to meet at Annapolis for the purpose of "revising the federal system and correcting its defects," Washington was placed at the head of the Virginia delegation. When the delegates met, he was unanimously called to the chair as president. This convention was in session for four months, and the result of its work was the Constitution of the United States as it now stands, with the exception of the amendments made in later years.

As Washington delivered his brief opening remarks to the delegates who assembled at the Constitutional Convention, he stated, "Let us raise a standard to which the wise and honest can repair; the event is in the hand of God."

During the year 1788, the Constitution was adopted by a sufficient number of states to make it effective. In the first election, Washington was chosen President and John Adams vice president for a term of four years beginning March 4, 1789.

Washington immediately began to prepare his affairs for leaving home. His farewell visit to his aged mother at Fredericksburg was touching and solemn because she was suffering with a painful disease to which she would soon succumb. On April 16, as he says in his diary, he "bade adieu to Mount Vernon, to private life, and to domestic felicity."

His progress to New York was a continued ovation. All along the route he was welcomed by addresses, the ringing of bells, and the thunder of artillery. He was very deeply touched by his reception at Trenton. As he approached the Delaware, where twelve years before he had crossed through drifts of floating ice in storm and darkness, he now saw a triumphal arch, which bore this inscription, "The defender of the mothers will be the protector of the daughters." At the bridge, the matrons of the city were assembled to do him honor, and as he crossed the bridge young girls, dressed in white and crowned with garlands, cast flowers before him, singing an ode expressive of their gratitude.

At New York his reception was royal. He was welcomed by Governor Clinton and conducted with military honors to a residence which was placed at his disposal. The streets and houses were beautifully decorated, and the crowd was so great that it was with difficulty that the city officers could make a way for the procession. Washington, preferring to go on foot, bowed right and left as he passed through the cheering multitude.

The inauguration took place with great pomp and ceremony on April 30, 1789. The oath of office was administered by Chancellor Livingstone, of the State of New York, upon a balcony in front of the Senate chamber and in view of the multitude. As the oath of office was administrated, Washington placed his hand on the Bible and swore to uphold and defend the Constitution of the United States and to faithfully execute the duties of his office. Moments later, he quietly added the comment, "So help me, God." Washington then delivered his inaugural address in the Senate chamber; after which, he walked with the whole assemblage to St. Paul's Church, where suitable prayers were read by the bishop of New York.

On May 17, Mrs. Washington, accompanied by her grandchildren, set out from Mount Vernon in her carriage to join her husband at the seat of government. There she presided over the household with the good breeding of one accustomed to directing the affairs of a hospitable home in the "ancient Dominion."

At first, the President was so overrun with visitors that he found it necessary to appoint fixed hours for their reception, thus freeing himself for his official duties. Many troublesome

questions of etiquette arose as to how the President should conduct himself. How should he appear in public? What kind of entertainments should he give? What title should he bear? All knew what a king should do, but who before had ever been called upon to act as President of a republic? At last, Congress decided that the chief magistrate should have no other title than that of his office, namely, "President of the United States," and the ceremonies of the office were made as few and simple as possible.

Hardly had these matters been settled before the President became sick. For weeks he was very ill; and when, at length, he was able to take up his duties again, many noticed that he had aged perceptibly. While still recovering from his illness, he received the news of his mother's death at Fredericksburg in her eighty-third year.

In September, Washington formed his cabinet, nominating Mr. Jefferson, secretary of state; General Knox, secretary of war, and Alexander Hamilton, secretary of the treasury. The new government was soon surrounded by trials and difficulties. The question of the national debt was the most important to be solved. Hamilton resolved that this debt should be paid in full and, supported by the President and Congress, he succeeded in providing for its payment.

ALEXANDER HAMILTON

In the autumn of 1790, troubles arose in the Ohio region with the

Miami Indians. General Harmar and General St. Clair, commanding separate armies, were both outwitted by the Indians and defeated with great loss. In 1793, General Wayne was sent by the President to the scene of action, and soon gained a great victory at Fallen Timbers. This victory broke the power of the Indians and they were compelled to sue for peace.

During his first term of office, the President made two tours through the country—one through the New England states and the other through the Southern states. He was much pleased by the visible return of prosperity and by the tokens of love and esteem which were showered upon him by the people as he journeyed along.

While on his southern trip, he selected the present site of the city of Washington. In 1790, the seat of government was moved from New York to Philadelphia for a period of ten years; after which, in the year 1800, it was to be established in the new city—Washington.

The discussion over the numerous measures of the first term had divided the people into two great political parties, the Federals and the Anti-Federals, or Republicans, later called Democrats. The former, headed by Hamilton, approved of a strong central government, while the latter, led by Thomas Jefferson, were opposed to those who wanted the Constitution to be amended to give more power to the general government at the expense of the individual states. Washington was much concerned to note this party spirit, for it disturbed not only the tranquility of the country but even the harmony of his cabinet. A true patriot, he knew no North, no South, no East, no West, and could not sympathize with the discontent.

The measures of the first administration, however, were so popular that, in 1792, Washington—now in his sixty-first year—was again elected President and John Adams vice president. The second administration of Washington began with serious troubles and complications. There were violent dissensions between the two great political parties; the war upon the frontier was still raging; and there were various troubles among the states. All these difficulties, however, were over-shadowed by foreign complications.

Since 1789, France had been convulsed by one of the most horrible revolutions known in history. Rising in their might to gain freedom from one form of tyranny, the people had gone beyond the bounds of God's law and had committed outrages that shocked the world. So radical and wicked had been their measures that they had beheaded their good king, Louis XVI, and imprisoned the generous Lafayette, the friend of Washington. Now, involved in war with England and Hol-land, the French republic was eager to form an alliance with the United States.

Washington was naturally grateful to France for the help she had given during the War for Independence, but he knew that such an alliance would be fatal to the infant American republic, which it was his duty to protect. Therefore, he issued a proclamation of neutrality, declaring that the United States would continue friendly relations with all contending nations. He also forbade Americans to aid any one of them.

In spite of the proclamation, Edmond Charles Genêt, the French minister, attempted to induce American citizens to espouse the cause of France, and behaved in such a manner that Washington was compelled to request his recall by the French government. These two actions raised a howl of indig-nation from the Anti-Federalists, who reviled the President for not siding with France, and accused him of sympathizing with Great Britain, and even of designing to be made king.

To add to this commotion, a new trouble arose. The distill-ers of western Pennsylvania refused to pay the tax upon whis-key levied by Congress and seized the officers sent to enforce the law. Washington immediately sent into those regions a strong military force under General Henry Lee (Light Horse Harry) to establish law and order. At the approach of this force the rioters dispersed, and the Whiskey Rebellion, as it is called, was ended.

In spite of all the wise measures of the government, a conflict between the United States and England now became imminent. To avert the horrors of another war, Mr. John Jay was sent to England to negotiate with the British government. He was successful in making an honorable treaty. The terms of the treaty were, however, very distasteful to the Anti-Federalists, and they determined that it should not be ratified. Public meetings were held, and orators harangued the people. Never before had the President been subjected to such a storm of malice and slander. His residence was even approached by a mob, who hooted and threw stones at it as an indication of their wrath and disapproval. But Washington, believing the treaty to be just and hoping to avert war, signed it in June, 1795.

It was well for the young republic that it had at the helm a pilot so prudent and bold as Washington. After the passions of the hour had subsided, it was seen that his measures had been wise and good, and once more he resumed the ascendancy over the minds of his countrymen. About this time, Mr. Jefferson, his brilliant political foe, wrote of him to Mr. Monroe, at Paris, thus: "Congress has arisen but to no avail. You will see by their proceedings the truth of what I told you, viz., that one man outweighs them all in influence over the people, who support his judgment against their own and that of their representatives. Republicanism resigns its vessel to the pilot."

But the pilot was now growing old and needed rest. When the period for the presidential election drew near, he was strongly urged to permit the use of his name for a third term. He had determined, however, to retire from public life, and in September 1796, he issued to the people of the United States his farewell address, a document filled with godly wisdom and patriotism. It made a profound impression upon the people, and hushed all suggestions of a third term.

On December 7, Washington met both houses of Congress for the last time. In his speech he advocated an institution for the improvement of agriculture, a military academy, a national university, and a gradual increase of the navy. In conclusion, he congratulated Congress upon the success of the government and implored upon the nation the blessings of the Supreme Ruler of the universe—Jesus Christ.

On March 4, 1797, Mr. Adams was inaugurated as the new President, and Mr. Jefferson vice president. When Washington, who was present at the ceremony, moved towards the door, the hall was filled with acclamations of love and respect. Upon reaching the street, he waved his hat in response to the cheers of the multitude, and departed, his eyes filled with tears, his emotion too great for utterance.

First in the Hearts of His Countrymen

Once again we find our beloved Washington at the "home of his heart," Mount Vernon. But now the hand of time has touched both master and home. The master has silvery locks, and his step is not so bold as when, a young ambassador, he crossed the "Great Divide." The house, which has remained unoccupied for several years, is falling into decay.

Washington found pleasure in making the necessary repairs to the mansion, and in having a building erected wherein to preserve his most important papers. He soon began his former routine of mounting his horse after breakfast and riding through his plantation until dinner, when, as he wrote to a friend, "I rarely miss seeing strange faces, come, as they say, out of respect to me."

So many visitors began to frequent Mount Vernon that he found it necessary to have someone to assist him in entertaining. He therefore wrote to his favorite nephew, Lawrence Lewis, then aide to General Knox, and invited him to make Mount Vernon his home—telling him frankly that by taking off his hands those duties which hospitality obliges one to bestow on company, he would render him a very acceptable service.

Mount Vernon was particularly attractive to the young gallants of the time; for Miss Nellie Custis had now grown up into a lovely woman. For some time it was not known which of her admirers was the favored one, but at last, to Washington's great satisfaction, she chose his nephew, Major Lawrence Lewis. Miss Nellie had inherited her grandmother's beauty and lively spirit and was a great favorite with the general. We are told that Washington was fond of children, especially girls; as to boys, with all his spirit of command, he found them at times somewhat ungovernable. "I can govern men," he would say, "but I cannot govern boys."

One evening, after Miss Nellie had been wandering alone by moonlight in the groves of Mount Vernon, she was given by her grandmamma a severe reproof for her reckless conduct. She admitted her fault and made no excuse, but when grandmamma made a pause in her lecture she left the room. As she was closing the door, she heard the general, who was walking up and down the floor with his hands behind him, say, "My dear, I should say no more—perhaps she was not alone."

Miss Nellie at once returned and, with a firm step, advanced to the general. "Sir," said she, "you brought me up to tell the truth, and when I told grandmamma that I was alone, I hope that you believe that I was alone."

The general made one of his most courtly bows and replied, "My child, I beg your pardon."

On February 22, 1799, Miss Custis was married to Major Lewis in the long drawing room at Mount Vernon. The mansion was decked with flowers and evergreens. All the gentle folks of the surrounding country attended the wedding, and the scene was one of great brilliancy and beauty. The occasion was especially gratifying to Washington.

In the midst of this poetic life, Washington was disturbed by the fear of a war with France. The troubles with that country had become so serious that the government voted an army, ordered a navy, and authorized our merchantmen to arm themselves against French men-of-war.

The President, Mr. Adams, wrote to Washington and entreated him to place himself once more at the head of the army. Before Washington could reply, the Senate had chosen him commander in chief of all the armies raised or to be raised. After some hesitation, he consented to accept the position on the two conditions that he should not be compelled to take the field unless there should be actual invasion, and that he should have the right to name his own subordinates.

Washington once more established his headquarters at Philadelphia, where he spent five weeks in consultation with other officers. He then returned to Mount Vernon, leaving the greater part of the responsibility to be borne by Major General Hamilton.

The American frigates put to sea and, in the summer and fall of 1799, did good service for the commerce of their country. The reorganization of the American army also went on and was soon completed.

In the meantime, however, the great Napoleon made himself First Consul of France. One of his first acts was to make overtures of peace to the United States. These were accepted, and in September 1799, a new treaty was made between the two republics.

Hardly was the war cloud scattered, however, before winter frosts and snow set in. Washington, in full health and strength, kept up an active interest in attending to his estate. On December 10, he finished a complete system by which his farms were to be managed for several years. It filled thirty folio pages and shows the soundness and vigor of his mind, as well as his love of order and good management.

The next day, after writing a letter to Hamilton, he mounted his horse and rode to a distant part of his estate. Before he reached home late in the evening, snow set in followed by a cold rain. Mr. Lear, his secretary, met him upon his return and, noticing that snow was hanging from his hair, expressed the fear that he was wet; but the general replied that his great coat had kept him dry. As dinner was waiting, he sat down to the table without changing his clothes.

On the following morning, he complained of a sore throat, but in the afternoon, he went out to mark some trees that were to be cut down. That evening, he was cheerful and calm, though a little hoarse. He sat in the parlor with Mrs. Washington and Mr. Lear and read the newspaper that had just come by post. During the night of December 11, however, he became quite ill with chills and had difficulty breathing.

The next morning, his old friend Dr. Craik was summoned to Mount Vernon to assess the former President's condition. He decided to send for a physician, but also instructed a servant by the name of Rawlins to bleed Washington.

From medical journals and records that were kept by the attending physician, we can reasonably deduce why George Washington's health went so quickly from bad to worse. These records reveal that Washington was bled so many times within a short period that his stamina was literally taken from him due to extreme blood loss.

His condition, therefore, became so serious that two additional physicians were summoned. These doctors, however, could not reverse the damage that had already been done by way of excessive bleeding procedures, and, in fact, probably never realized the connection between such procedures and Washington's critical state.

Silent and sad, his physicians sat by his bedside looking on him as he lay panting for breath. They thought about the past, and tears soon welled in their eyes. Washington noticed their tears and, stretching out his hand to them and shaking his head, said, "O, no! don't! don't!" then with a delightful smile added, "I am dying, gentlemen, but thank God, I am not afraid to die."

The next day, he lay in and out of consciousness and was overheard saying, "I should have been glad, had it pleased God, to die a little easier, but I doubt not it is for my good."

Feeling that the hour of his departure out of the land of the living was at hand, he requested to be left alone for a time so he could commune with his Maker. At length, he said: "I am going soon. Have me decently buried; and do not let my body be put into the vault in less than three days."

Around ten o'clock that evening, he made several attempts to speak before he could finally manage to utter his last words, "Father of mercies, take me to Thyself." Minutes later, the great statesman and Christian patriot, George Washington, went to be with his Lord and Savior Jesus Christ.

The news of his death touched all with heartfelt grief. Many, as a symbol of their sorrow, put on dark mourning clothes. Congress, upon receiving the sad intelligence, went in funeral procession and mourning garb to the German Lutheran church where General Henry Lee, in a touching oration, declared that the departed general had been, "First in war, first in peace, and first in the hearts of his countrymen."

When the news reached England, Lord Rudport, commanding sixty vessels of the line, lowered his flags to half-mast; and Napoleon, First Consul of France, ordered that emblems of mourning be suspended from all standards for the period of ten days, pronouncing at the same time a beautiful tribute to the virtue of "the warrior, the legislator, and the citizen without reproach."

Washington died on December 14, 1799, in the sixty-eighth year of his life. The funeral was simple and modest, according to his wishes—all confined to the grounds of Mount Vernon which, "after forming the poetic dream of his life, now became his final resting place."

When his will was read, one of the first provisions was found to direct, upon the death of Mrs. Washington, the freeing of his slaves. He had long been resolved never to purchase another slave. Indeed, for some time his mind had been filled with anxiety for the future of his beloved country. He felt that in the course of time the institution of slavery would bring about civil strife. In a letter to Major Lewis in 1797, he said, "I wish from my soul that the legislature of the State would see the policy of a gradual abolition of slavery. It might prevent much mischief."

Another provision of his will provided that a copy of one of his personal Bibles be given to Bryan Lord Fairfax, along with notes given to Washington by Rev. Thomas Wilson, bishop of Sodor and Man.

When Mrs. Washington learned from her husband's will that he desired the emancipation of his servants, she at once relinquished her legal right over them and set them free. She also requested that the vault in which her husband's remains had been placed should not be sealed; for, said she, "It will have to be opened soon." Her prediction was quite accurate, as she outlived her illustrious husband by only a little more than two years.

Mount Vernon was willed by General Washington to his distinguished nephew, Bushrod Washington, who, leaving no children, bequeathed it to his nephew, John Augustine Washington. From his hands, the mansion and fifty acres of land, in 1858, passed into the keeping of the Mount Vernon Ladies' Association. It was then dedicated to the people of the United States, and is kept as a monument whither all lovers of true liberty may go to gain inspiration.

As we review the life of Washington we notice especially the uprightness, modesty, and steadfastness of his character. It cannot be shown that he consistently practiced a single vice, and his modesty was surpassed only by his courage. When depressed by defeat, discouraged by the inadequate support of Congress, or distressed by the condition of his starving and mutinous soldiers, had he once faltered, the "flower of liberty" would have perished in the bud, and the colonies would have remained, at least for a time, under the dominion of Great Britain.

No one of sound judgment and proper information will deny Washington a place among the great military leaders of the world. As an organizer, we see him at Boston transforming the mob of citizens and farmers into trained soldiers; as a strategist, we find him at Trenton and Princeton entrapping the enemy by his wonderful maneuvers; and as a brave impetuous leader, we admire him at Princeton and Monmouth, spurring to the front and rallying his men to victory.

But the capstone of Washington's character was his virtuous patriotism. At first, Congress watched him with a jealous eye, fearing that he might assume too much power. They soon found, however, that their commander in chief watched their interests more closely than his own—that their liberties were entirely safe in his keeping. His pure love of country was soon recognized, not only in America but across the ocean; and there is no doubt that the character and dignity of the American commander influenced in no small degree the French government to enter into a treaty of alliance with the United States.

Washington the general was a great man, but Washington the President was even greater. Wise, beneficent, steadfast, and incorruptible, he guided the republic through the stormy years of her infancy and was yielded to God is his imperfect efforts to place her among the nations of the earth. His faculties, taken separately, were not the most brilliant, but they were so evenly balanced as to constitute a genius of the highest order. The superb evenness of his nature was nowhere exhibited so plainly as in his Christian faith. He accepted the simple biblical faith taught at his mother's knee—refusing to parade his faith around as some sort of external show. Many of his letters, and especially his first inaugural address, show an abiding faith in the Christian religion. The way in which

he faced death was also a strong indication of his personal faith in the God of the Bible.

And now, though more than two centuries have elapsed since Washington was laid in the silent tomb, his reputation and legacy still shines brightly in the memory of all true patriots, and he is still "first in the hearts of his countrymen."

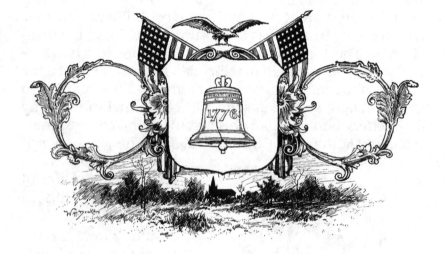